Rickard's Record

Cardiff and the Valleys - Volume 1

Brian J Miller

The Wider View

PREFACE

So who needs this book and its companion, volume two? Well, anyone with an interest in Sid Rickard's photography in South Wales, obviously, but the volumes go beyond the simple theme of photograph albums. Historians and steam railway enthusiasts will find much of interest since the photographs were taken between forty and fifty years ago. Railway modellers may appreciate the potential offered by prototypical cramped layouts, short platforms, busy freight workings, short trains, sidings galore, almost every excuse for a lineside industry and, in some cases, almost bizarre operating practices.

Operating information, or the lack of it, has often been commented upon in the modelling press. This book, like its forthcoming companion volume, is not a treatise on 'operation' by any stretch of the imagination but, as well as photographs, offers an insight into how the freight traffic in the Cardiff District was moved in the 1950s, the instructions governing its movement and what the trains looked like.

Tony Miller
Wider View

Edited and typeset by Tony Miller, Great Gidding

Printed in Great Britain by Stylaprint, Ailsworth, Cambridgeshire

Bound by Woolnough's, Irthlingborough, Northamptonshire

Published and distributed by The Wider View, 2 Luddington Road, Great Gidding, Huntingdon, PE28 5PA.

Front cover ....
There is an urge to jump clear as No.6647 approaches St. Fagans station with the 10.15am Crockherbtown-Briton Ferry Class H goods on Saturday, 4th April 1953. The photograph appears inside as Plate 66.

.... Rear cover
The bunker of No.5627 nearing Taffs Well and showing target J7, an unusual shape. This Down mineral train is an Abercynon duty and the photograph, from Plate 13, was taken on Monday, 10th March 1958.

Further Reading ....

- *For historical detail, and to discover how and why so many small companies competed in such a small area, 'A Regional History of the Railways of Great Britain, Volume 12, South Wales' by D S M Barrie, published by David & Charles 1980, is highly recommended. The same publisher's 'Forgotten Railways, South Wales' by James Page, 1979, complements the 'Regional History'.*
- *'Rails in the Valleys' by James Page, published by David & Charles, 1989, affords a valleys overview, as the title suggests.*
- *For additional pictorial detail of South Wales in broadly the same era as that covered by this volume, Michael Hale's six-volume 'Steam in South Wales' series is unsurpassed and particularly comprehensive. The first four volumes were published by Oxford Publishing Company, volumes five and six by the Welsh Railways Research Circle.*
- *The series of 'Track Layout Diagrams of the Great Western Railway' by R A Cooke, published by the author, and his 'Atlas of the GWR 1947' (Wild Swan 1988) are essential aids for unravelling the complexity of the routes and junctions of inter-connecting lines, yard and industrial layouts. The Diagrams and Atlas aid the understanding of the relevant operating instructions, too.*

.... and Further Research

If you need help or guidance with research into Welsh railways, contact the Welsh Railways Research Circle either by visiting the group's web site at www.wrrc.org.uk or through the publisher at editor@widerview.co.uk.

CONTENTS

ACKNOWLEDGEMENTS

To Richard Harman for the use of the base maps from which all the maps used herein have been derived, and to the British Railways Board for permission to use extracts from the 1950 Sectional Appendix.

USING THIS BOOK

Information Sources

All the local freight and mineral train details relating to each depot have been extracted from the BR(W) Working Timetable, Section G (Cardiff District Branch Lines), effective between 16th September 1957 and 8th June 1958.

Where possible, operating details or restrictions in force at the mineral trains' destinations are noted in the photographic pages. These details have been extracted from the 1950 Sectional Appendix and are displayed in panels throughout the book. The verbatim instructions from the Appendix are prefixed by ●; locations and topics are noted in the Index.

Representative locomotive allocations have been collated from a number of sources.

Abbreviations

Not all trains ran every day or at the same times each day. The rail system often eased into a new week with different timings on Mondays from those for the rest of the week; other trains might not run on Saturdays as the week drew to a close.

MO - Mondays Only; MX - Mondays Excepted; SO - Saturdays Only; SX - Saturdays Excepted were the most common abbreviations, the other days being represented by Tu, W, Th, F and Su. In this book, + means 'Runs if required'.

TRAIN and TRAFFIC WORKING - the CONTROL

Train and Traffic Control

In most railway writings, little attention is paid to the role of the Control Office in expediting traffic flows, making adjustments to the train service to reflect the daily variation in the amount of traffic on offer, dealing with a 'stop' on some types of traffic or coping with the aftermath of an accident. A number of the freight turns worked by each shed depended on Control Office instructions for some or all of their work for that particular day. Since there are frequent references to Control, a selection of instructions has been gleaned from the 1950 Sectional Appendix to highlight the Office's functions.

GENERAL INSTRUCTIONS

- No departure must be made from the booked working without the authority of the Controller.
- It will be the duty of the Train Controllers to keep in close touch with all points and control the working generally, i.e. see that traffic from Collieries, Works, Junctions, etc., is promptly cleared; Trains loaded as nearly as possible to their full capacity; light mileage avoided as far as practicable; unnecessary shunting eliminated; overtime avoided whenever possible, and the Trains got over the roads at times which are most suitable to prevent delay.
- They must pay particular attention to the dispatch of urgent coal for immediate shipment or urgent empties or pitwood for Collieries due to shortages, and to Trains conveying such traffic having due priority.
- They must also keep themselves informed and advise all concerned of the working and loading of Freight Trains at places outside the Control Area, with which they can communicate by telephone.
- No special Train must be ordered or extra trip run without the Traffic Controllers' previous consent, and all special power required for shunting or Goods Train working must be ordered through them.
- Advices to be sent to Controllers. - All messages with reference to the regulation of empty wagons for the various Collieries must be sent direct to the Control Office, and the latter is responsible for advising all concerned as to the stopping, releasing, or hurrying forward of empty wagons.
- In addition, a daily advice shewing the state of all Colliery and Works Sidings, giving particulars of traffic waiting clearance, of Colliery Empties then on hand, also requirements for the night and following day's work, must be sent to the Control Office at 3.0 p.m., or as near that time as possible.
- Besides the special advices and the daily report at 3.0 p.m. referred to in the preceding paragraph, advices must be sent to the Control Office of all traffic immediately it is ready for clearance.
- All stop and release orders, whether applying to coal, pitwood, Colliery Empties or any other traffic, to be immediately notified to the Control Office.
- The loading and departure of all Trains must be notified to the Control Office from the starting depot, and all points where the Trains pick up. The arrival times at terminating points must also be advised.
- Any exceptional delay in connection with yard working to be specially reported to the Controller. Also delays to Trains (including Light Engines and Vans) in running from any cause, ie., waiting Assisting Engine, at Signals, etc. Trains must be reported under their Set Numbers, but if the Signalman is not aware of the Set Number, the Engine Number must be given.
- Station Masters and others in charge of Train Depots must send to the Controllers the earliest possible intimation of cases of Trains required to be stopped or run at other than the booked times owing to illness of Trainmen or other cause.
- Working of Assisting Engines, and Engines from Sheds.- The working of all Assisting Engines will be under the control of the Controller, and he must be advised as soon as it is known a Train will require an Assisting Engine between any points, so that arrangements may be made in good time to provide assistance. When an Engine has finished assisting a Train the Controller must be consulted as to its subsequent movements.
- Working of Cattle Traffic, and Traffic in exceptional quantities.- All cattle traffic, special consignments, or traffic in exceptional quantities about to pass must be promptly advised to the Controller, and also when it is likely that there will be insufficient traffic on hand for any particular service.
- Traffic blocked back. - In sending advices of Goods traffic blocked back, details of the various classes of traffic for each Station or Works must be specified.
- Accidents. - Any accident in the Division whereby the working over any running Line is affected, or any mishap inside a Yard, for which the Breakdown Gang will be required, or that is likely to cause serious delays to succeeding Trains, must be immediately reported to the Controller, so that any convenient diversion or other special working arrangements may be promptly made ....
- Relief for Enginemen and Guards. - All applications for relief for Drivers and Guards required to be given in the Control Area must be made to the Control Office, where the necessary arrangements will be made in conjunction with the Locomotive Department.

SIDNEY RICKARD
1920 - 1996

*"Dear Mr Rickard, I would like to order the following
140 prints from your catalogue."*

So started a friendship of some twenty years. Much to my regret we never met but, through weekly correspondence, I feel I came to know the man who had the foresight to record the railway scene of the 1950s and 1960s for posterity. Not only were the main line workings taken into account but also the branch lines which held such a fascination for him.

During early correspondence I recall asking, "Why did you spend so much time in the Valleys?" "Because nobody else was," came the reply.

Sid started taking railway photographs about 1951, mixing with the likes of John Hodge and Bob Tuck, with whom he became very good friends, the pair of them spending days together at the lineside, improving their techniques all the time.

With the locomotives of the former pre-grouping railways of South Wales fast disappearing, Sid took it upon himself to record their passing, his favourite engines being those of Rhymney Railway ancestry. The opportunity to photograph them in their everyday surroundings was taken whenever the opportunity arose, be it in rain, sun or snow.

By his own admission, Sid was not a railway enthusiast in the true sense of the term; he was 'a railway photographer', a subtle difference. Plans for visiting locations were made in advance by checking through working timetables and maps of the area. A preliminary visit was made to the site to find the best vantage point for photographing the workings. With this information gathered, he would then set out, possibly the following week, to capture the scene for all time. Such planning was essential as train movements at some of the locations visited were very infrequent indeed, yet a pannier tank or whatever caught on film with the local goods at a backwater setting gave more satisfaction than reels of film of main line engines

It was during these early years that the technique of capturing railways in the landscape, rather than just locomotives, was adopted and now, with so much of the railway infrastructure gone forever, we can look back to the days that some of us can remember well; the pick-up freight, the single coach auto-train, the seemingly endless flow of mineral trains and so on, as seen through the lens of Sid Rickard, a good friend. This book is a tribute to him.

Brian J.Miller
Barry, April 2002

1

INTRODUCTION

Welcome to the first volume of *Rickard's Record* which, through the photographs of the late Sidney Rickard, illustrates locomotive workings of depots in the Cardiff Valleys Division during the 1950s and early 1960s. Due to the complexity of the working arrangements for the period covered, it was decided early on that the volumes in this series would give an outline of the duties undertaken by the various depots in the Division, along with the locomotives that were used. Should the reader seek to expand on this information, Working Timetables and Appendices are available from time to time from secondhand book dealers specialising in transport material. The Welsh Railways Research Circle, too, can be highly recommended as a source of information.

In this volume, the depots in the Cardiff area are covered as well as those at Abercynon and Barry. The next volume will deal with the depots at the heads of the valleys and those at Llantrisant and Tondu, thus photographically covering the whole of the Division. No apology is made for the inclusion of some previously published prints as it was felt that, by their omission, the theme of the book would suffer.

The formative years

A glance at a railway map of South Wales prior to 1963 shows a myriad of lines all seemingly side by side. This is not the case, however, as in most instances there were mountains between each line or, as in the Rhymney Valley, there was a railway on each side. These lines had been built by the former local pre-grouping companies, such as the Taff Vale, Rhymney, Barry and Cardiff Railways which exported principally through the ports at Cardiff and Barry.

The Brecon & Merthyr, Pontypridd, Caerphilly & Newport (PC&N) and Alexandra (Newport & South Wales) Dock & Railways (ADR) companies exported further east, through Newport docks.

Obviously, the earlier the railway company was established, the easier the route from the coastal ports to the coalfields as far as gradients were concerned, for the surveyors could choose the best path for the railway.

Late-comers, such as the Barry, were faced with no alternative but to build lofty viaducts to cross the valleys and to reach the coalfields by securing running powers over other company lines, the only option open as all the possible routes using the valley floor had been used. Even so, the expenditure on the construction of these routes was nothing compared to the profits to be had from the transportation of coal to the South Wales ports, hence the proliferation of lines in the area.

Apart from the PC&N, each company had its own engines and engine sheds at strategic points along their routes for the movement of coal from the various collieries, passenger traffic (which was usually a secondary consideration), the return of empty wagons and the import of material such as pit-props.

At the Grouping in 1923, coal was still being exported in vast tonnages although, since the heady days prior to the First World War, these figures had begun to decline. Even so, the traffic was still significant enough to warrant the Great Western Railway rebuilding many of the engine sheds of the pre-grouping companies and deciding to construct a class of 200 locomotives specifically for South Wales coal traffic. Now that the GWR had the coal monopoly, some routes which relied on using running powers to reach the collieries were closed as they were no longer needed now that all lines were now owned by one company. Likewise, a rationalisation of locomotive depots took place with some being closed and their engines transferred to other depots in the area. It was in this vein of slow decline that traffic flows continued right through to the late 1950s and early 1960s.

Operations and traffic

Although many of the lines in the South Wales area were heavily graded, generally speaking the gradients assisted the train in that it was mainly empty trains that had to climb them. Loaded trains had to contend with falling gradients, which was not without its hazards. The vast majority of the locomotives allocated to the depots were of the tank engine style, so turntables were not needed at their home sheds although there were exceptions. The pre-grouping companies had set the precedent of locomotives working up the valleys chimney first, a practice that continued right through to the 1950s.

To give some idea of the amount of traffic handled in the South Wales Division in the 1950s it may be a surprise to learn that nigh on one and a half thousand engines, or roughly two-fifths of the entire Western Region stock, were allocated to depots in the 86, 87 and 88 shed-code areas. In the Cardiff valleys the 0-6-2T wheel arrangement was very popular and its ancestry can be traced back to the pre-grouping companies. However, traffic movement was not totally reliant on this type; many trains, both passenger and freight, were handled by engines of the 0-6-0PT arrangement, which was found to be ideally suited for working the lighter trains over tortuous routes.

Not only was there north to south traffic, but also east to west via the main line and the Vale of Neath line. The

Pontypridd, Caerphilly and Newport line, too, was an ideal route for traffic from the valleys destined for England. For instance, the Abercwmboi to Severn Tunnel Junction freights, worked by Aberdare engines and crews, were routed that way.

With that number of movements, it is not surprising to find that a lot of the freight trains would only average between five and eight miles per hour, and obviously if the engine was required to shunt at the various yards en route the average speed would drop even lower. Freight trains also had to have their own 'paths' whereby they could fit in between passenger trains. This was not a problem on the quadruple track sections but delays were inherent on the double and single line sections, this being known as the 'knock on effect', whereby one late train could delay, say, the next half a dozen or more if they were tightly scheduled.

Some of the freight duties, even over relatively short distances, were manned as double turns, whereby the engine would leave the shed with one crew and return some fifteen or sixteen hours later with another crew, the first set of men having been relieved part way through the duty.

During the period covered by this book, even with rail traffic being in slow decline, it was still a logistical nightmare to try and find paths for extra trains such as special freights, extra passenger workings and so on.

Passenger timings appear to be slow compared to the distance covered but it must be remembered that there were stations every few miles and, to keep to the timings, some smart running between stations was called for, part of the reason why tank engines with their small diameter wheels were the preferred choice.

Generally, the stock for these trains was marshalled in five coach rakes though this would be strengthened during peak periods. If there were parcels vans for any of the terminus stations such as Treherbert or Merthyr, they would be attached to passenger trains.

Another important factor was the inter-connection of passenger trains, especially at places such as Pontypridd which offered services to Caerphilly and Machen, Cardiff,

Barry via Wenvoe, Cardiff via St. Fagans, Ynysybwl, Treherbert, Merthyr and Aberdare. Everything had to work like a well oiled machine or the system would be brought into disarray.

At various junctions along the routes, large interchange sidings had been built by the pre-grouping companies for the handing over of coal traffic from one company to another or for the marshalling of this traffic. Stormstown Junction, Treforest Junction, Aber Junction, Roath Branch Junction and Radyr Junction to name but a few, and all were still busy places during the 1950s. Wherever you went in the valleys at this time, there were lots of trains.

The photograph collection

Bearing the foregoing in mind, it is not hard to see the appeal that the area had for Sid Rickard. Engines could be seen working very hard, there were passenger trains, auto-trains, pick-up freights, industrial settings, shunting engines. banking engines; in fact, apart from a greater variety of locomotives, the valleys offered everything that the main line could. That aside, the important factor was that few photographers were recording the slow decline and that is why Sid took it upon himself so to do. Many photographers would, perhaps, have found train after train with different tank engines at their heads uninspiring; thankfully for us, Sid did not. In fact, the area was a source of inspiration to him and a lot of time was spent searching out the best vantage points from where the railways could be photographed going about their everyday work. Those sites often included industrial backdrops or wooded hillsides that gave depth to his photography, so that the picture was not just a shot of the engine, which most of us have been guilty of at sometime or another.

There were no crack expresses on these lines, no fast freights - in fact, nothing prestigious at all. An operating area where the skill of the enginemen was not in getting a train going, but in trying to stop it. Now, thanks to the efforts of Sid Rickard all those years ago, we can look back on the scenes that were taken for granted.

Plate 0 - The ex-Taff Vale Railway signal box on the Down platform at Sully. Saturday, 23rd March 1957

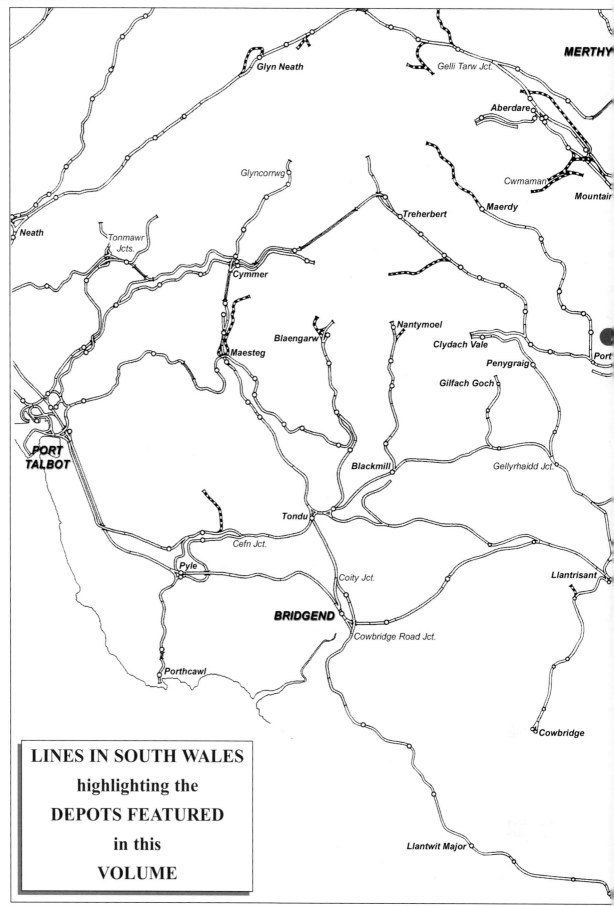

MERTHY

Glyn Neath

Gelli Tarw Jct.

Aberdare

Cwmaman

Mountair

Glyncorrwg

Treherbert

Maerdy

Neath

Tonmawr Jcts.

Cymmer

Nantymoel

Blaengarw

Clydach Vale

Port

Penygraig

Maesteg

Gilfach Goch

Blackmill

Gellyrhaidd Jct.

Tondu

Cefn Jct.

Coity Jct.

Llantrisant

Pyle

BRIDGEND

PORT
TALBOT

Cowbridge Road Jct.

Porthcawl

Cowbridge

LINES IN SOUTH WALES

highlighting the

DEPOTS FEATURED

in this

VOLUME

Llantwit Major

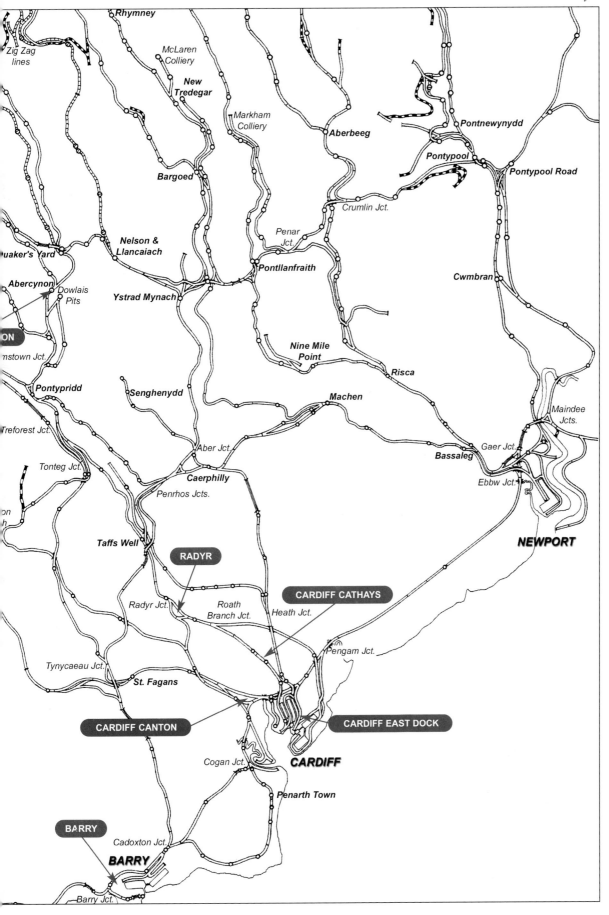

Rhymney
Zig Zag lines
McLaren Colliery
New Tredegar
Markham Colliery
Aberbeeg
Pontnewynydd
Pontypool
Pontypool Road
Bargoed
Crumlin Jct.
Penar Jct.
Cwmbran
Nelson & Llancaiach
uaker's Yard
Pontllanfraith
Abercynon
Dowlais Pits
Ystrad Mynach
Maindee Jcts.
nstown Jct.
Nine Mile Point
Risca
Pontypridd
Senghenydd
Machen
Treforest Jct.
Aber Jct.
Gaer Jct.
Bassaleg
Ebbw Jct.
Tonteg Jct.
Caerphilly
Penrhos Jcts.
on h
NEWPORT
Taffs Well
RADYR
CARDIFF CATHAYS
Radyr Jct.
Roath Branch Jct.
Heath Jct.
Pengam Jct.
Tynycaeau Jct.
St. Fagans
CARDIFF CANTON
CARDIFF EAST DOCK
Cogan Jct.
CARDIFF
Penarth Town
BARRY
Cadoxton Jct.
BARRY
Barry Jct.

88E   *ABERCYNON*

Abercynon, designated 88E, was a two-road dead-end shed adjacent to the up end of Abercynon Station. It was a Great Western Railway replacement for a smaller Taff Vale Railway shed that stood at nearly the same location but closed on 2nd November 1964.

In the winter of 1957/58, the shed was responsible for the working of 12 mineral and goods turns, described below.

Target No.	Start time; time off shed	Start point, destination and notes + - Runs if required
J6	**6.0am MX** Off shed 5.55am; **5.0am MO** Off shed 4.55am;	Work Abercynon Van Siding to Black Lion etc. MX, Maesmawr etc. MO 16hrs double turn; J6 (Relief) to clear Pontcynon Jct. at approx. 5/40pm.
+J8	**6.30am** Off shed 6.25am;	Work Abercynon Van Siding to Stormstown Jct., Lady Windsor Colliery, thence as ordered by Control. 16hrs, relieved 1/30pm. Work trip Treforest Trading Estate to Radyr Jct.
J11	**9.5am** Off shed 9.00am;	Work Abercynon to Cwm Colliery
J12	**11.50am** Off shed 11.45am;	Work Abercynon Van Siding to Penrhiwceiber
J16	**4/10pm SX** Off shed 4/05pm;	Work Abercynon Van Siding to Marshalling Sidings
CK	**6/25pm SX**	Work Stormstown Jct. to Nantgarw and Roath Branch Jct.
J17	**7/10pm SX** Off shed 7/05pm;	Work Abercynon Van Siding to West Mendalgief or R&SB Jct.
J20	**10/0pm SX** Off shed 9/55pm;	Work Abercynon Van Siding to Dare Valley Jct.
X2	**6.45am** Off shed 6.10am;	Work Coke Ovens to Eirw Branch Jct. and Llantrisant
X10	**9.50am** Off shed 9.0am;	Work Coke Ovens to Treforest Estate
+X13	**2/30pm** Off shed 2/10pm;	Work as ordered by Control
+X16	**5/0pm SX** Off shed 4/40pm;	Work as ordered by Control

---

Locomotives allocated to Abercynon during 1957 included:

0-6-2T Nos.304, 349, 365, 370, 373, 381, 383, 390, 393, 397, 398
0-6-0PT Nos.1610, 1620
0-6-0PT Nos.3650, 3707, 3727, 3730, 3734, 3783
0-6-0PT Nos.4601, 4626, 4631, 4672, 4686
0-6-2T Nos.5601, 5617, 5618, 5623, 5627, 5630, 5641, 5643, 5680, 5682, 5686, 5699
0-6-0PT Nos.6411, 6435, 6438
0-6-0PT Nos.7733, 7744
0-6-0PT Nos. 9642, 9769, 9776

SHUNTING and BANKING TURNS.

Abercynon provided one engine for banking duties, on duty at 6am Mondays until 6am Sundays. The duty, JP1, also covered shunting at Abercynon and Stormstown but with a short break between 9pm and 10pm when the engine visited the shed. On Saturday evenings it worked a 10/30pm trip to Coke Ovens (Pontypridd).

There were two other shunting duties - JP5, a single-manned turn that shunted Abercwmboi for 7½ hours, seven days a week, and X10, already noted above, that shunted 6 hours a day from 10.15am (4 hours on Sundays) at Treforest Estate.

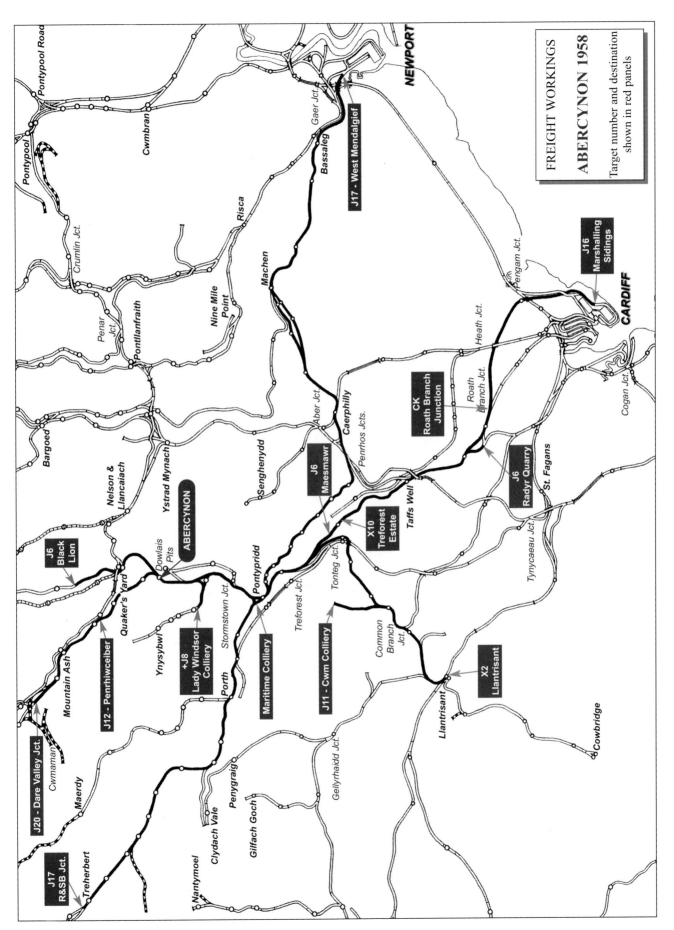

FREIGHT WORKINGS
ABERCYNON 1958

Target number and destination shown in red panels

7

Plate 1 - The business end of No.398, at Abercynon shed on Saturday, 3rd August 1958, the same month as its withdrawal. No.398 was built by Hawthorn Leslie for the Taff Vale Railway as Class A No.409.

(Right) Plate 3 - Abercynon's No.5641 departing from Taffs Well Station with the 11.0am Merthyr-Barry Island stopping passenger train on Thursday, 3rd March 1955. If the coal in the top of the bunker is anything to go by, the fireman is going to be busy with the hammer.
The amount of steam leakage evident on the front end of the engine points to leaking glands, so it is not suprising to see that No.5641 entered Barry Works on 19th September 1955 for overhaul when she received the boiler (No.2261BA) from engine No.6671. No.5641 was returned to traffic on 14th November 1955. The trackwork visible above the second coach is the Walnut Tree Junction to Penrhos Junction line, known locally by railwaymen as 'The Big Hill' because of the 1 in 47 gradient, often necessitating the use of a banking engine, normally supplied by Radyr Shed.

(Above) Plate 2 - No.5686, a long-term resident of Abercynon, in 'light' steam outside her home shed and looking resplendent in lined green livery. The roof of Abercynon station is just visible to the right behind the 0-6-0PTs. The date is Saturday, 3rd August 1957.

(Above) Plate 4 - No.6411, one of Abercynon's auto-fitted pannier tanks, draws into Nantgarw Halt with the 2/52pm Pontypridd-Machen auto-train on Tuesday, 4th September 1956, having traversed the former PC&N route on a service to be withdrawn from 17th September. Other auto workings covered by Abercynon included Pontypridd-Cardiff (Clarence Road) via St.Fagans, Cardiff (Bute Road)-Coryton, Abercynon-Aberdare and Cardiff (Clarence Road)-Penarth. No.6411 was scrapped at Caerphilly Works in June 1961.

(Below) Plate 5 - Former Taff Vale Railway 0-6-2T No.304 (ex-TVR No.412 and GWR No.402) in rebuilt form, is seen in a fairly clean condition but out of steam on her home shed of Abercynon on Saturday, 3rd August 1957. This locomotive was withdrawn the same month.

Plate 6 - No.398, a former Taff Vale Railway Class A engine which retained the round top water tanks when rebuilt by the GWR. Formerly TVR No.409, No.398 was dealt with at Caerphilly Works in July 1930. The engine is seen here shunting at Maritime Colliery, Pontypridd, working Abercynon's XP3 duty, which was a pilot turn based at Coke Ovens (Trehafod). The bridge in the background carried the former Barry Railway main line from Cadoxton to Trehafod. Tuesday, 12th June 1956.

CARN PARC SIDINGS.

No.5601 and its train shown in Fig.7 is standing at the water column on No.3 Up Siding. The Appendix notes that the siding was used as a running line from Stormstown Junction to Carn Parc Sidings. Water for Down trains was available on the Down Relief line.

Plate 7 - No.5601 of 88E taking water at Carn Parc Sidings, near Abercynon, whilst employed on the J6 Up goods. The engine had been here previously in the day with empties from Stormstown Junction to Black Lion Siding (for Merthyr Vale Colliery) and would have picked up the Abercynon's JP1 banking engine at this location for the climb up the valley. Tuesday, 12th January 1960.

Plate 8 - No.5641 arriving at Abercynon station with the 11.0am Merthyr-Barry Island passenger train, the JD target indicating that this is another Abercynon duty. The Aberdare branch can be seen diverging to the left at the junction. The engine shed was situated to the right of the picture. Saturday, 3rd August 1957.

The 11.0am Merthyr-Barry Island

Plate 9 - Another view of the same service, though this time behind No.5643 and passing Upper Boat power station carrying target JD, of Abercynon. No.5643 was withdrawn in July 1963 and was to pass into preservation in September 1971. Thursday, 25th October 1956.

Plate 10 – A summer's evening in 1957 sees No.373, of 88E, heading along the Roath Branch with the J16 6/55pm (SX) Marshalling Sidings-Stormstown Sidings empties. No.373 was originally Taff Vale Railway No.139 and had been rebuilt by the GWR at Swindon Works in March 1926 but retained the TVR round top tanks. Although looking in good external condition the locomotive would be withdrawn in less than two months time. Tuesday, 25th June 1957.

Plate 11 - No.5682 brought to a halt by signals at Carn Parc whilst working the J12 12/40pm Penrhiwceiber Lower Junction-Radyr Quarry Junction mineral train on Tuesday, 12th January 1960. No.5682 would then work a train of empties from Radyr Junction, departing at 2/35pm, to Stormstown Junction. With the amount of steam issuing forth from the rear of the cab it is possible that a boiler gauge glass has blown.

ABERCYNON to QUAKER'S YARD - Working of the Main Incline.

Railways in the valleys were blessed by steep inclines - the Appendix listed gradients steeper than 1 in 200 - and special instructions were issued for train working and for use of assisting engines. The Main Incline between Quaker's Yard (LL) and Abercynon included lengths at 1 in 38, 1 in 42 and 1 in 80 and some of the Working Instructions are noted here.

● The speed of Trains descending the incline must be limited as shewn below, viz:- Passenger Trains, Engines and Vans, or Light Engines not to exceed booked passenger speed. Freight and Mineral Trains 8 miles an hour.

● Extra Vehicles on Passenger Trains for Merthyr District. When extra vehicles are attached for the Merthyr district, an advice must be sent from the starting point to Abercynon at least an hour before the departure of the Train by which the vehicles are sent, in order that arrangements may be made for an assisting Engine to be in readiness to assist the Train to Quaker's Yard (L.L.). When there are no extra vehicles on a Train the assisting Engine is not to be kept at Abercynon to assist Up Passenger Trains, but must be utilised under the instructions of the Control Office.

● Up Freight Trains may, when necessary, be assisted over the incline with two assisting Engines in the rear. In the cases of Trains coming from the Aberdare Branch with traffic for Quakers *(sic)* Yard Junction, and requiring the assistance of one or more assisting Engines to ascend the Main Incline, it will not be necessary to run round the Brake Van at Abercynon. In such circumstances the Guard must ride upon the assisting Engine, or upon the first assisting Engine, should two be necessary.

● On the Main Incline, between Quaker's Yard (L.L.) and Abercynon, an Engine, or an Engine with Van only, may be attached either in front or at the rear of a Down Freight Train if worked by a single Engine, and the two Trains, or Train and Engine, may proceed coupled together as one Train through the section.

● If in the opinion of the Driver an Assisting Engine is required to ensure the safe descent of any Train with the ordinary load for one Engine, and in every case in which such ordinary load is exceeded, he must, on approaching Black Lion, give 6 short whistles. The Black Lion Signalman must advise the Controller, who will make arrangements to provide an Assisting Engine. A Guard must accompany the Assisting Engine from Abercynon and assist the Train Guard in applying hand brakes.

Plate 12 - No.5699 in clean condition climbing the 1 in 69 gradient from Treforest Junction to Tonteg Junction with the J11 10.2am Treforest Junction-Cwm Colliery empties, the engine having left Abercynon with a brakevan at 9.5am. Saturday, 13th October 1956.

(Right) Plate 14 - High noon at Tonteg Junction as No.5680 of 88E is about to descend the 1 in 69 gradient to Treforest Junction with the J11 11.52am Cwm Colliery-Maritime Colliery mineral train. The reason for taking coal to another colliery was for blending purposes, whereby the produce from different pits could be mixed together to form a certain type of fuel. Evident in this photograph is the fact that the guard has already been along the train and 'pinned down' the required number of wagon brakes ready for the descent ahead; they would then be lifted at Treforest Junction. The locomotive is on the former Taff Vale Railway route from Llantrisant whilst to the left the former Barry Railway main line from Cadoxton to Trehafod skirts the hillside. The date is 25th October 1956.

MARITIME and PENRHIW COLLIERY SIDINGS, PONTYPRIDD.

The train in Plate 14 is destined for Maritime Colliery, Pontypridd, for which special instructions were in force for some Down trains:

● This Siding has a connection with the Up Rhondda Line. The entrance to the Siding is on a sharp curve and the gradient rising towards the Colliery is very steep. Trainmen must exercise great care when putting Wagons in and taking them out. Those which remain on the Siding must in all cases be firmly secured.

● A board is fixed to indicate a point beyond which Engines must not pass.

● Down Trains conveying more than 12 wagons of coal for Maritime Colliery must be brought to a stand at Pontypridd Junction Box clear of the crossover road leading from the Down to the Up Main Line.

● The Coke Ovens Shunting Engine, which the Controller must arrange to arrive at Pontypridd in advance of the train, must then be attached to the rear of the Train, and with an Engine at each end, the whole will. be crossed to the Up Main Line.

● The Train Engine must be detached and taken clear of the Colliery connection, whilst the Coke Ovens Shunting Engine propels the Wagons into the Colliery Sidings.

● Guards of Up Trains on the Relief Line having traffic to detach in Maritime or Penrhiw Sidings must be careful to leave the rear portion of their Trains clear of the Crossings from the Up Main to Relief near Maritime Siding, and in every case they must satisfy the Signalman at Pontypridd Junction as to the exact position of the Train.

● When picking up traffic from Penrhiw Colliery Siding, the Guard or Shunter in charge of the Train must, before drawing out of the Siding on to the Main Line, pin down a sufficient number of brakes to steady the Train and keep the couplings taut. Drivers must draw out carefully.

Plate 13 - No.5627 nearing Taffs Well with a Down mineral train on Monday, 10th March 1958 and carrying target J7, an Abercynon duty. Owing to the amount of traffic using the line, the Taff Vale Railway had to quadruple the track between Pontypridd and Cardiff in an attempt to alleviate the congestion.

(Below) Plate 15 - Two years later and No.5680 passes Pontcynon Junction with a brakevan returning from Dare Valley Junction to Abercynon Van Sidings. The lines in the background were for Nixon's Colliery. The former TVR Pontcynon Junction signal box would appear to be a bit on the draughty side if the sheets hanging in the windows are anything to go by. However, the signalman does have an adequate supply of coal outside the box even if the lumps are a little on the large side. Friday, 10th October 1958.

Opposite page
(Upper) Plate 16 - No.6438 of 88E easing out of Tonteg Halt with the 12/45pm auto-train from Cardiff (Clarence Road) to Pontypridd via St. Fagans on Thursday, 25th October 1956. The engine would be carrying the JB target.

(Lower) Plate 17 - Another of Abercynon's former Taff Vale Railway Class A 0-6-2Ts. Driver Morgan is in charge of No.390 as it stands at Tonteg Halt waiting to set back to Treforest Junction after having banked a Down freight train over the route. Note that the locomotive still has the round top tanks and carries the XP2 target. No.390 would be withdrawn in this month. Wednesday, 14th August 1957.

(Below) Plate 18 - Caerphilly station witnessing the arrival of No.5641 with the 3/0pm Cardiff (Bute Road)-Quaker's Yard (High Level) stopping passenger train on Friday, 13th August 1954. This engine spent most of its life in the Abercynon area before it was withdrawn in September 1964. This is thought to be the only photograph that Sid took of an Abercynon engine working in the Rhymney Valley.

ORIENTATION of ENGINES at ABERCYNON SHED.

● As far as practicable, Engines with or without Brake Vans should reach the Abercynon Sheds when finishing duty with the chimney leading up line, and Drivers are authorised, when they have to pass Stormstown on their way to shed, to travel over whichever curve at Clydach Court will enable them to bring Engines into Shed in the desired position, provided it can be done without involving delay. Facilities must be given for this to be done.

● To enable the above to be carried out, Engines may propel Brake Vans between Clydach Court and Abercynon provided the Guard is riding in the Van.

WORKING at STORMSTOWN.

● No.6 Up Siding and No.6 Down Siding at Stormstown are used as Running Lines for Up and Down Trains respectively, and are under the control of the Foreman, or person in charge. The Signalman at Stormstown or Carn Parc, as the case may be, must obtain permission from the Foreman, or person in charge before admitting a Train to these Sidings.

WORKING of TRAFFIC, ABERCYNON COLLIERY.

● Traffic for Abercynon Colliery must be propelled from Stormstown, the Guard or Shunter riding on the leading vehicle or preceding it on foot to keep a sharp look-out and signal the Driver.

● The train must be brought to a stand at the gate leading to the Colliery Sidings, and the Shunter must proceed to the top end of the Main Line Sidings (as far as the Weighing Machine) to see that the crossings are clear and the points properly set.

(Above) Plate 19 - Having not long left St. Fagans station, No.6401 accelerates a Pontypridd-Cardiff (Clarence Road), via St. Fagans, auto-train towards Cardiff on Saturday, 14th May 1955, the JB target confirming that it is an Abercynon working. The section between the stations at Ely (Main Line) and St. Fagans is very picturesque and Sid Rickard took some excellent photographs along there.

(Below) Plate 20 - Tonteg Halt with No.5699 approaching working the X2 11.0am Llantrisant-Coke Ovens freight on Thursday, 25th October 1956. The engine would enter Barry Works on 14th December of that year for new tyres and axleboxes.

Plate 21 - It is Friday, 10th October 1958 and No.5627 is at Pontcynon with an Up train of 'duff' for the Phurnacite Plant at Abercwmboi. Note that the 'J Special' target is displayed.

(Above) Plate 23 - No.5686 entering Merthyr Vale station with the 1/0pm Barry Island-Merthyr stopping passenger train, the return working of the 11.0am Merthyr-Barry Island service; note the JD target. Thursday, 6th March 1958.

(Above) Plate 22 - Another shot of Abercynon's No.6438, this time at Penarth Town station waiting to propel an auto-train to Cardiff. The engine would have worked down to Cardiff (Clarence Road) earlier in the day with an auto-train from Pontypridd, after which it would work the Clarence Road-Penarth auto service before returning to Pontypridd via St. Fagans. No.6438 spent quite a number of years allocated to 88E although it was withdrawn from Laira shed in November 1962 and scrapped at Cashmores of Newport in November 1964. The photograph was taken on Saturday, 20th April 1957.

(Opposite page)
Plates 24 and 25 - Two elevated views off Taffs Well showing the railway layout in the area. The top view is taken from the eastern side of the valley with an 82xxx 2-6-2T approaching Taffs Well bunker first with a Down passenger train. The line in the foreground is from Walnut Tree Junction to Penrhos Junction, behind that is the line into Nantgarw Colliery and at the rear is the Cardiff to Pontypridd line. The upper picture was taken on Saturday, 19th October 1957.
The lower view is taken from the western side of the former Barry Railway Walnut Tree viaduct with Walnut Tree Junction in the foreground and a 56xx 0-6-2T coming off the line from Penrhos Junction. The former Barry Railway route to Penrhos Junction can be seen skirting the hillside in the background. This view is looking up the valley; the Cardiff to Pontypridd line running right to left and the line to Nantgarw Colliery branching off to the left of the picture. The former Rhymney Railway engine shed at Walnut Tree Junction is visible in the foreground behind the short rake of wagons in the siding. Saturday, 11th July 1959.

88C   *BARRY*

Barry, shed code 88C, was a shed of six through roads and had been constructed by the Barry Railway Company as its main locomotive depot. Apart from alterations to increase the available headroom, there were no major alterations prior to closure on 10th September 1964.

In the winter of 1957/58, the shed was responsible for the working of 20 mineral and freight turns, described below.

Target No.	Start time; time off shed	Start point, destination and notes + - Runs if required
B5	**6.20am** Off shed 5.40am;	Work Cadoxton to Lady Windsor Colliery
B13	**4.45am MX** Off shed 4.25am; **6.30am MO** Off shed 6.10am;	Work Barry Sidings to Coity Junction (Double trip)
+B7	**6.30am** Off shed 6.15am;	Work Barry Van Siding as ordered by Control
B6	**7.0am** Off shed 6.20am;	Work Cadoxton to National Colliery
B15	**7.35am** Off shed 6.35am;	Work Barry Sidings to Aberthaw and Cardiff (16 hours)
B16	**8.55am** Off shed 8.15am;	Work Cadoxton to Tymawr Colliery
B34	**9.15am** Off shed 8.55am;	Work Barry Sidings to Coity Junction
B10	**10.0am** Off shed 9.15am;	Work Cadoxton to Penallta Colliery
B24	**11.40am** Off shed 11.0am;	Work Cadoxton to Mountain Ash
+B20	**6/45pm** Off shed 6/30pm;	Work Barry Van Siding as ordered by Control (Margam and return)
B21	**12/35pm** Off shed 11.55am;	Work Cadoxton to Penrhiwceiber
B26	**1/0pm** Off shed 12/20pm;	Work Cadoxton to Lady Windsor Colliery
B25	**2/0pm** Off shed 1/5pm;	Work Cadoxton to Penallta Colliery
B29	**3/5pm** Off shed 2/35pm;	Work Barry Sidings to Coity Junction
B31	**3/45pm** Off shed 3/05pm;	Work Cadoxton to Peterston (also Aber Junction SX)
B40	**6/45pm SX** Off shed 6/15pm; **5/0pm SO** Off shed 4/30pm;	Work Barry Sidings to Coity Junction (Double trip)
B36	**6/35pm SX** Off shed 6/15pm; **5/20pm SO** Off shed 5/0pm;	Work Barry Goods Yard to Cardiff (Newtown)
B41	**7/30pm SX** Off shed 6/50pm; **5/10pm SO** Off shed 4/20pm;	Work Cadoxton to Peterston (SX) Work Cadoxton to Aber Junction (SO)
B42	**9/0pm SX** Off shed 8/10pm; **6/30pm SO** Off shed 5/45pm;	Work Cadoxton to Ystrad Mynach (SX) Work Cadoxton to Aber Junction (SO)
B43	**11/15pm SX** Off shed 10/55pm;	Work Barry Goods Yard to Treforest Junction via Radyr Junction

---

SHUNTING ENGINES.

No shunting turns are noted in the timetable for Barry engines. That, however, merely relates to shunting at stations and yards outside the docks. Pilot engines would work as required in Barry Docks moving traffic to and from the sidings at Cadoxton and Barry Sidings.

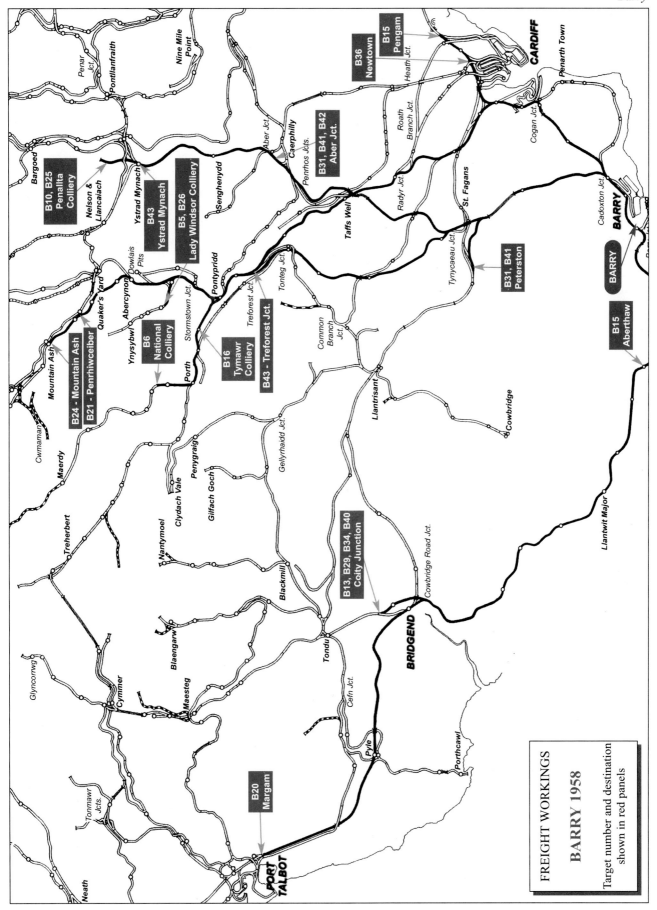

FREIGHT WORKINGS

BARRY 1958

Target number and destination shown in red panels

(Above) Plate 26 - On Tuesday, 5th April 1955 No.5529 of 88C is seen departing from Creigiau Station with the 9.55am auto-train for Cardiff (Clarence Road). The engine had worked the 9.30am service from Cadoxton, arriving at Creigiau at 9.48am, which allowed just seven minutes for passengers to detrain and for No.5529 to shunt the stock into the Down platform before it was time to depart for Cardiff via St. Fagans.

(Below) Plate 27 - No.5614 was allocated to Barry throughout the 1950s and is seen here to the east of St. Fagans with the Barry B40 turn, which was the 6/45pm Barry Sidings-Coity Junction empties. This train was booked to travel over the Vale of Glamorgan line but would from time to time travel via Penarth Curve and the main line, as in this instance on Wednesday,12th June 1957, probably due to traffic using the Vale of Glamorgan route.

Plate 28 - Arguably this must be one of the finest photographs of a train crossing the former Barry Railway viaduct at Walnut Tree. On Saturday, 19th October 1957 Barry resident No.5609 is working the B10 10.0am Cadoxton-Penalltau Junction empties past the Steetley Dolomite Works, which appears to be in full production. The locomotive spent the majority of her working life at Barry and was withdrawn in October 1964. It was through this narrow gap in the valley that the lines of the former Taff Vale and Cardiff Railways ran, along with the Glamorgan Canal, the River Taff and two roads. The only route left for the Barry Railway, which was a relative late-comer on the scene, to reach the coalfields of the Rhymney Valley was to build this magnificent viaduct and cross from one side of the valley to the other to gain access to the Rhymney Valley via Penrhos Junction.

Plate 29 - Looking north at Tynycaeau Junction on Thursday, 6th June 1957 as No.6643 approaches at the head of the B6 10.0am National Colliery-Cadoxton Yard mineral train. The lines diverging to the left in the background were for Creigiau, Efail Isaf, Tonteg and Trehafod whilst those to the right were for Penrhos Junction.

WORKING BETWEEN COWBRIDGE ROAD JUNCTION and COITY SIDINGS.

There are numerous instructions for working this stretch of railway, mostly dealing with communication between individuals, so only the instructions relevant to train movements are reproduced here.

● The Up and Down Lines between Cowbridge Road Junction and Coity Sidings are worked by telephone communication. The persons in charge of the working are the Signalman at Cowbridge Road Junction and the Shunter in charge at Coity Sidings.

● Trains from the direction of Coity, having work to do at Cowbridge Road Junction, must stop short of the Up Branch Home Signal, leaving sufficient room for the engine and any wagons which may have been picked up in the sidings, to be set back on to the train with the engine outside the Home Signal.

FREIGHT TRAINS PUT OFF AT TYNYCAEAU.

● In the event of a Train or portion of a Train being left on the Up or Down Relief Lines, a swing tail lamp must be placed on the last vehicle by the Guard who places the wagons on the Relief Line.

DOWN RELIEF LINE, DOWN SIDING, AND GROUND FRAME AT CREIGIAU.

● The Down Relief Line and the Down Sidings at Creigiau will not accommodate Trains of more than 40 wagons, and the Signalman at Tonteg Junction must advise the Signalman at Creigiau when a Down Train of 40 wagons or less passes Tonteg Junction Signal Box.

● Ground Frame. - Trainmen, when requiring to let a Train out, must reverse No.1 lever, pull over No.3 (which is for the points), then pull over No.2 (which controls the slots in the Signals). This will allow the Signalman to pull off the "Starting" Signal. After the Train has passed out of the Siding, No.2 lever must be put back, then No.3, after which No.1 must be pulled off. The latter is the "Starting" Signal, and shows also that the levers have been put back and the Lines set for the Main Line. Drivers must not start away until they have received the Signal from the Guard that he has joined the Train.

WORKING OF TRAINS OVER UP and DOWN GOODS LINES BETWEEN BARRY JUNCTION and BARRY SIDINGS SIGNAL BOXES, and VICE VERSA.

● Two through Sidings are set apart for the working of Up and Down Freight Trains.

● No Train must be allowed to enter the Up Goods Line from Barry Sidings Box until the Signalman has received an assurance from the Yard Foreman at Barry Sidings that all handpoints are properly set for its safe passage.

● No train must be allowed to enter the Down Goods Line from Barry Junction until the Signalman has been informed by the Yard Foreman what Siding it is to enter, and the Signalman has given this information to the Trainmen.

● Wagons may be propelled over the respective lines from either end, and the Guard or Shunter will be responsible for preceding the vehicles on foot or riding in a suitable vehicle at the front of them and signalling to the Driver to stop short of any obstruction or of a converging line.

● Trains working over these lines, or vehicles being propelled, must not exceed a speed of eight miles per hour.

(Above) Plate 30 - This general view of the front of Barry shed was taken from the Up end of Barry station on Sunday, 14th April 1957. No.4673 was allocated to Southall at the time and had received a heavy overhaul at Barry Works, being fitted with the boiler from No.5778 in the process. No.82041 had also been into the Works for repairs, which included some welding to the right-hand water tank.

(Below) Plate 31 - No.4610 taking water at Barry Sidings working the B15 2/0pm Aberthaw West-Pengam goods. This was quite a heavy train conveying cement from both the Aberthaw and Rhoose Cement Works and would have required the guard to pin down the brakes of the wagons before the train descended the 1 in 81 gradient of Porthkerry Bank. The shunter's pole leaning against the rear buffer of the engine indicates that the guard has just been around the train and lifted all the brakes off now that the foot of the bank has been reached. The date is Friday, 29th August 1958 but, in the following January, No.4610 left South Wales for a foray onto the Southern Region, being allocated first to Folkestone followed by spells at Feltham, Weymouth and Exmouth Junction prior to withdrawal in October 1964.

(Below) Plate 33 - No.5619 departing from Dingle Road Halt with the 2/40pm Penarth Town-Merthyr stopping passenger train, part of the Barry BE turn, on Thursday, 23rd October 1952. This locomotive was a long term resident of Barry and on 12th June 1951 had been in a serious accident at Walnut Tree Junction whilst working the B10 1/0pm Penrhiwfelin-Cadoxton Yard mineral train. Instead of travelling via Walnut Tree Viaduct the train had been diverted via 'The Big Hill', Penrhos Junction to Walnut Tree Junction route, whereby, on descending the bank, it was found that the engine could not hold the train back so, with increasing speed, the engine and train were sent into the sand drag at Walnut Tree Junction. Although No.5619 stayed upright, considerable damage was done to the wagons with quite a few being reduced to matchwood. Until that time No.5619 had always been considered a 'strong' engine but after the impact, which resulted in the engine having a twisted frame, performance was mediocre. The locomotive was withdrawn in June 1964 and, after a period at Woodhams scrapyard on Barry Docks, passed into preservation in May 1973.

(Left) Plate 32 - Walnut Tree Viaduct as seen from Taffs Well; one of Barry's 56xx 0-6-2Ts is crossing the viaduct with the BI0 10.0am Cadoxton Yard-Penalltau Junction empties. The lines in the foreground led into Nantgarw Colliery. Saturday, 10th November 1956.

Plate 34 - A 56xx 0-6-2T with a Down mineral train for Cadoxton Yard crossing the former Barry Railway's Tynycaeau Viaduct. The Cardiff to Swansea main line is in the foreground while the St. Fagans to Tynycaeau Junction single line passed under the bridge on the right of the picture. Friday, 20th February 1959.

SPECIAL INSTRUCTIONS FOR WORKING TRAINS OVER STEEP INCLINES
Penrhos Junction and Walnut Tree Junction.

● The speed of Down Trains must not exceed eight miles an hour upon any part of the Nantgarw incline, and when two Engines are provided for Trains passing down the incline, both Engines must be in front of the Train.

● All engines and trains travelling in the down direction must be brought to a stand at Walnut Tree Junction Home Signal, at the foot of the incline, and the brakes must not be released or unpinned nor the Engine put in gear nor the Engine or Tender brake slackened, until the Junction Signal has been lowered for the Train to proceed through the Junction.

● An Indicator is provided on the Down Branch to Relief Inner Home Signal to show the number of trains in the Section on the Down Relief Line between Walnut Tree Junction and Pentyrch Crossing. The Signalman will be responsible for working the Indicator. If the Section is not clear, a green hand signal must be exhibited to the Driver as the Train passes the Signal Box.

CADOXTON SIDINGS.

● The Sidings extending from Cadoxton South Junction to Cadoxton North Signal Box are accessible at both ends - those situated on the Up Line side are for the reception of wagons from the Docks, and those situated on the Down Line side are for the reception of loaded wagons off Down Main Line Trains.

● Trainmen working into these Sidings must satisfy themselves that wagons are not left foul of the crossings at either end of the Sidings.

● In ordinary circumstances Down Main Line Trains will terminate at the Cadoxton Sidings. The Engine and Train will be taken into one Siding; the Brake Van will be uncoupled and travel by gravitation to the South end of the Sidings, clear of the Crossings.

● Unless instructions are issued to the contrary by the Inspector, No.6 Siding must be used for Brake Vans and No.1 Siding for Pilot Engines.

● Light Engines, Engines and Vans, or short Trains requiring to cross between the Down Sidings and Up Main Line should, as far as possible, be worked through the Crossover road between the Down Sidings and Up Main Line.

● The Junction leading from the Down Sidings to the Cogan Branch Line will serve Down Sidings Nos.12 to 18 and the Up Bay Sidings. Trains departing from these Sidings will be able to proceed through the Cadoxton Bay Line to East Dock Storage sidings High Level.

● As far as possible, Down Main Line Trains conveying traffic for East Dock should be placed on Down Siding Nos.12 to 18, so that the greatest possible use may be made of this Junction.

(Above) Plate 35 - No.5621 was another engine that spent quite a time allocated to Barry. It is seen here passing the staggered platforms of Ystrad Mynach station with the B10 10.0am Cadoxton Yard-Penalltau Junction empties on Saturday, 7th September 1957. The line here is on a 1 in 145 rising gradient, of which No.5621 seems only too well aware.

(Below) Plate 36 - It was not only steam workings that carried target numbers. Two 3-car DMUs approaching Taffs Well on Monday, 10th March 1958 provide a Down service for Barry Island, the first unit displaying the BB target denoting a Barry working. Judging by the condition of the units they would appear to be new since the lead set is not yet adorned with the 'cat's whiskers' warning stripes .

(Above) Plate 37 - No.82030 was allocated to Barry from new but only spent four months allocated there, being transferred to Shrewsbury in May 1955. In this view, taken on Thursday, 3rd March 1955, No.82030 is leaving Taffs Well station with the 9.0am Aberdare (Low Level)-Barry Island passenger train, part of the Barry BF turn. The lines diverging to the right are for Penrhos Junction whilst the sand drag that arrested the runaway No.5619 referred to in the caption for Plate 33 is visible on the right of the picture.
(Below) Plate 38 - Another 2-6-2T allocated to Barry was No.4163, here drawing into Dingle Road Halt with a Down passenger working carrying the BP target on Thursday, 23rd October 1952. The line from Cogan Junction to Penarth Town suffered a rising gradient of 1 in 45, so pulling away from Dingle Road Halt could sometimes be difficult.

(Above) Plate 39 - *The severity of the rising gradient between Cogan Junction and Penarth Town is evident in this view of a 56xx 0-6-2T passing through Penarth Dock station with a Down passenger train on Thursday, 23rd October 1952.*
(Below) Plate 40 - *A 56xx from Barry shed skirts the mountainside above Glan-y-Llyn with a train of empties from Cadoxton Yard to Penalltau Colliery on Saturday, 10th November 1956. This is the same train that appears in Plate 32.*

(Above) Plate 41 - No.5667 spent a number of years allocated to Barry and, on a bright September day in 1957, is approaching Ystrad Mynach station with a passenger train for Rhymney. Note that the engine is carrying the RA target denoting a Rhymney turn. The 0-6-2 wheel arrangement, synonymous with the Cardiff valleys, had been adopted by a number of pre-grouping railway companies and was found to be ideally suited to the work. After 1922, as these engines from constituent companies were passing through the various Shops of the GWR and private locomotive builders, it was found that a lot of the locomotives in question were beyond viable repair. That led to the introduction in 1924 of a new class of 200 0-6-2Ts designed by Collett for use in South Wales and numbered 5600-99 and 6600-6699. The reason for continuing the same wheel arrangement was that it had been so successful in the past and the 56xx class became 'maids of all work' in the area, covering all types of duties. The class in general was a good design, but they did suffer from hot axle boxes and there was a pronounced front to back oscillation at speed. The photograph was taken on Saturday, 7th September 1957.

(Below) Plate 42 - No.82044 running alongside the Rhondda Fawr near Porth with the 1/30pm Barry Island-Treherbert passenger train, which has a parcels van for Treherbert attached at the rear. With the line on a steady rising gradient and the apparent lack of any undue exhaust No.82044, carrying the BD target, would appear to be in very good condition. Saturday, 12th May 1956.

(Left) Plate 43 - No.82044 on the way back down the valley near Llwynypia with the 3/55pm Treherbert-Barry Island passenger train on that same Saturday, 12th May 1956. Note the small Taff Vale Railway cast iron trespass notice to the right of the engine and also that, during the run round period at Treherbert, the fireman has omitted to transfer the BD target to the bunker.

Locomotives allocated to Barry during 1957 included:

0-6-0PT No.1600
2-6-2T No.4578
0-6-0PT Nos.4601, 4610, 4692
2-6-2T Nos.5527, 5529
0-6-2T Nos.5609, 5614, 5619, 5621, 5648, 5664, 5667
0-6-0PT No.5769
0-6-0PT No.6408
0-6-2T Nos.6615, 6637, 6641, 6643, 6658
0-6-0PT Nos.6712, 6722, 6723, 6724, 6733, 6738, 6740, 6745, 6746, 6747, 6748, 6750, 6752, 6753, 6754, 6758, 6770, 6771
2-8-2T Nos.7230, 7241, 7252
0-6-0PT Nos.8437, 8446, 8450, 8459, 8465
0-6-0PT No.8735
0-6-0PT No.9453
0-6-0PT Nos.9622, 9631, 9676
2-6-2T Nos.82003, 82035, 82036, 82037, 82039, 82040, 82041, 82042, 82043, 82044

Plate 44 - Nigh on brand new but out of steam, No.82043 stands at the rear of Barry Shed on Tuesday, 19th July 1955. A former Taff Vale Railway Class A 0-6-2T can be seen outside the six-road shed; to the right is the ash shelter, built as a precautionary measure during the Second World War, and to the right of that the large coal stage. No.82043 is standing on one of the roads leading to the Fitters' Shop.

(Above) Plate 45 - Another engine to spend quite a number of years allocated to Barry Shed was No.6637, seen here carrying the BC target and departing from Abercynon station with a Barry Island-Merthyr passenger train on Saturday, 3rd August 1957.

(Below) Plate 46 - No.5632 displaying the BB target passes Roath Branch Junction with the 9.30am Barry Island-Treherbert passenger train on Friday, 9th April 1954. Enginemen working passenger trains in the Cardiff Valleys District were regarded as 'top link' and, though not carrying the same prestige in most people's eyes as, say, Canton, the crew had to be very competent due to short start-to-stop timings over heavily graded routes.

(Above) Plate 47 - Barry's No.8437 nearing Pontcynon with the B24 11.10am Cadoxton Yard-Mountain Ash Colliery empties, a round trip of some 47 miles. Water would be taken at Pontypridd Junction on the Up trip and at Abercynon on the Down. Friday, 10th October 1958.

(Below) Plate 48 - A general view of Barry Town station and junction on Friday, 29th August 1958. The DMU without the 'cat's whiskers' warning stripes in the Up platform had formed the 3/0pm (SX) Llantwit Major-Barry service and the DMU in the adjacent platform was the 2/46pm service from Cardiff. To the right of these is 0-6-0PT No.8450 and to the rear of that locomotive are the buildings which comprised Barry Works. On the right hand side of the picture the locomotive depot is visible and the extra brickwork added to the walls to give more headroom is apparent. The lines in the foreground lead to the Vale of Glamorgan, whilst those branching off to the right of the picture are for Barry Island.

YSTRAD MYNACH NORTH DOWN SIDINGS.

● Guards of Trains must not uncouple the brakevans until they are inside the Catch Points on the Down Relief at the entrance to the Down Sidings and clear of the Relief Line.

ARRANGEMENTS for WORKING CYLLA BRANCH TRAFFIC to AVOID RUNNING ROUND at YSTRAD MYNACH.

● Traffic from the Cylla Branch in Train loads for Hengoed may be worked forward from Ystrad Mynach North to Hengoed with the Assisting Engine in front, coupled to the Brake Van and the Train Engine in the rear of the Train, in order to avoid the reversing of the Van and Train Engine at Ystrad Mynach North.

● Similarly, full Train loads of traffic on Down Trains for Penalltau Colliery may be worked from Ystrad Mynach North with the Assisting Engine leading, coupled to the Van and the Train Engine acting as Assisting Engine in the rear.

● In each case one Guard must ride on the rear Engine.

PENALLTAU COLLIERY, CYLLA BRANCH.

● When wagons are propelled into the Sidings, care must be taken not to foul the connections at the Colliery end except by arrangement with the Colliery staff.

HENGOED (LOW LEVEL) EXCHANGE SIDINGS.

● The Siding nearest to the Up Line to Rhymney must, as far as practicable, be kept clear for use as a running line. Trainmen must satisfy themselves that it is clear before proceeding over it.

(Above) Plate 49 - On the evening of Saturday, 2nd July 1960, No.5664 of Barry shed was employed on the Coity Junction-Barry Sidings pick-up freight and is seen here setting back into Rhoose goods yard. It was just prior to this date that Barry changed their target letter from B to J, the pristine J21 target carried by No.5664 bearing testimony to the change.

(Right) Plate 50 - On Saturday, 7th September 1957, No.6641 has now completed shunting the B25 1/0pm Cadoxton Yard-Penalltau Colliery empties on the Cylla Branch and is propelling the brakevan towards the yard and onto a loaded train ready for the return journey to Cadoxton Yard. Note the former Rhymney Railway somersault signals in the foreground. When shunting operations were being carried out at this location, hand signals could not be seen because of the curvature of the track, so movements were controlled by a siren fixed to a signal post. The view is taken looking down the valley and the railway running above No.6641 is the Pontypool Road to Neath line.

88A   *CARDIFF CATHAYS*

C ardiff (Cathays), allocated 88A by British Railways, was a ten-road dead-end shed built by the Taff Vale Railway but improved on a couple of occasions by the GWR. The depot lost its shedcode in December 1957 when most of the engines were transferred to Radyr. Cathays closed to steam in July 1958, after which the servicing of DMUs was undertaken there until final closure in November 1964.

In the winter of 1957/58, the shed was responsible for the working of 24 mineral and freight turns, described below.

Target No.	Start time; time off shed	Start point, destination and notes + - Runs if required
C6	4.30am MSX Off shed 4.20am;	Work Cathays Van Siding to Cwmparc Colliery
C8	8.15am Off shed 8.05am;	Work Cathays Van Siding to Llanbradach
C10	4.45am MX Off shed 4.35am;	Work Cathays Van Siding to Penrhiwceiber (MX)
	5.50am MO Off shed 5.40am;	Work Cathays Van Siding as required (MO)
C12	9.30am Off shed 9.20am;	Work Cathays Van Siding to McLaren Colliery
C14	7.15am Off shed 7.05am;	Work Cathays Van Siding to Ferndale
C16	7.40am Off shed 7.30am;	Work Cathays Van Siding to Ocean Colliery
C18	8.20am Off shed 8.10am;	Work Cathays Van Siding to Treharris, Aber Junction and Nantgarw Colliery
+C19	6.30am Off shed 6.20am;	Work Cathays Van Siding to Roath Power, Tymawr Colliery and as ordered (16 hours)
C22	10.05am Off shed 9.55am;	Work Cathays Van Siding to Ferndale (Runs if required on Saturdays)
C24	11.10am Off shed 11.0am;	Work Cathays Van Siding to Elliot Colliery
C25	1/05pm Off shed 12/55pm;	Work Cathays Van Siding to Ystrad Mynach thence Ocean Colliery
C28	12/30pm Off shed 12/20pm;	Work Cathays Van Siding to Albion Colliery
C29	2/0pm Off shed 1/50pm;	Work Cathays Van Siding to Ogilvie Colliery
C30	2/30pm Off shed 2/20pm;	Work Cathays Van Siding to Black Lion
C31	4/0pm Off shed 3/50pm;	Work Cathays Van Siding to Elliot Colliery
C33	5/43pm SX Off shed 5/33pm;	Work Cathays Van Siding to Maerdy
C34	5/38pm SX Off shed 5/28pm;	Work Cathays Van Siding to Penrhos Junction thence Ocean Colliery, Treharris
C36	6/30pm Off shed 6/20pm;	Work Cathays Van Siding to Cwmparc Colliery
C37	6/15pm SX Off shed 6/05pm;	Work Cathays Van Siding to Aber Junction and Bargoed Pits
C38	8/40pm Off shed 8/30pm;	Work Cathays Van Siding to Stormstown
+C43	8/55pm SX Off shed 8/45pm;	Work Cathays Van Siding as required
---	10.15am Off shed 9.30am;	Work Crockherbtown to Margam
---	8/0pm SX Off shed 7/15pm;	Work Crockherbtown to Margam (return to Llantrisant)
CP8	10/0pm SX ---	Work Cathays To Radyr Junction and Roath Basin Junction (8 hours)

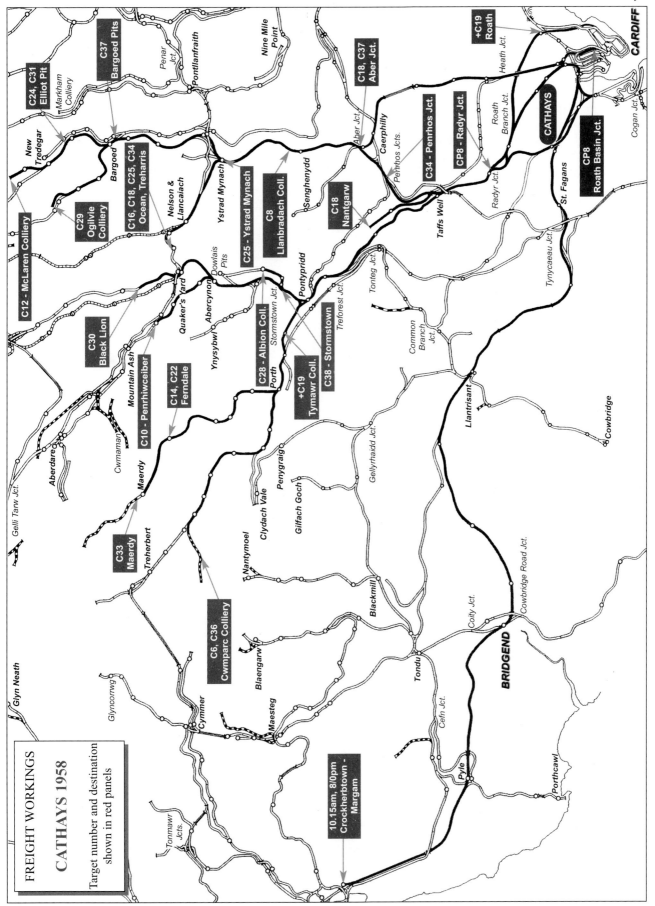

FREIGHT WORKINGS
CATHAYS 1958

Target number and destination shown in red panels

C24, C31 Elliot Pit

C37 Bargoed Pits

C12 - McLaren Colliery

C29 Ogilvie Colliery

C16, C18, C25, C34 Ocean, Treharris

C25 - Ystrad Mynach

C8 Llanbradach Coll.

C18 Nantgarw

C18, C37 Aber Jct.

+C19 Roath

C34 - Penrhos Jct.

CP8 - Radyr Jct.

CATHAYS

CP8 Roath Basin Jct.

C30 Black Lion

C10 - Penrhiwceiber

C14, C22 Ferndale

C28 - Albion Coll.

+C19 Tymawr Coll.

C38 - Stormstown

C33 Maerdy

C6, C36 Cwmparc Colliery

10.15am, 8/0pm Crockherbtown - Margam

Gelli Tarw Jct.

Glyn Neath

Aberdare

Cwmaman

Mountain Ash

Aberdare

Quaker's Yard

Abercynon

Ynysybwl

Dowlais Pits

Nelson & Llancaiach

Ystrad Mynach

Senghenydd

Bargoed

New Tredegar

Markham Colliery

Penar Jct.

Pontllanfraith

Nine Mile Point

Aber Jct.

Caerphilly

Penrhos Jcts.

Heath Jct.

Roath Branch Jct.

CARDIFF

Cogan Jct.

St. Fagans

Tynycaeau Jct.

Radyr Jct.

Taffs Well

Pontypridd

Stormstown Jct.

Porth

Treforest Jct.

Tonteg Jct.

Common Branch Jct.

Llantrisant

Cowbridge

Maerdy

Treherbert

Penygraig

Clydach Vale

Giffach Goch

Nantymoel

Blaengarw

Cymmer

Maesteg

Glyncorrwg

Tonmawr Jcts.

Blackmill

Tondu

Cefn Jct.

Coity Jct.

Cowbridge Road Jct.

BRIDGEND

Pyle

Porthcawl

Gellyrhaidd Jct.

43

Plate 51 - Former Taff Vale Railway Class A 0-6-2T No.391 (TVR No.405), allocated to Cathays for quite a number of years, is heading a Down mineral train along the Roath Branch on Saturday, 26th May 1956, just four months away from withdrawal. A fortnight prior to this, No.391 was one of the locomotives chosen for a Gloucestershire Railway Society tour of South Wales, No.2538 being the other.

CATHAYS LOCOMOTIVE YARD.

● There are two lines communicating with the Locomotive Sheds at Cathays, one at the North end and the other at the South end. Engines, with or without Brake Vans, are passed to or from the Shed through either of the lines which are signalled at both ends, and trapped at the ends nearest the Main Line.

● A post is fixed at the North end of Cathays Loco. Yard between the Van Siding and the running line to the Shed. This post is painted white, and after dark a lamp showing a white light in both directions is fixed upon it. The object of this post is to indicate the point beyond which Engines proceeding from the Shed must not pass until the Driver is satisfied either by personal observation or sending his Fireman forward, that the line ahead is clear. A Guard, in shunting out his Van upon the Coal Stage or Turntable Road, must not allow it to pass south of the post in question.

● Fog or Falling Snow. - To secure the safety of Engines passing to and from the Engine Shed during fog or falling snow, when the Signalman cannot see the Signals controlling Engines coming out, the Cathays Yard Master must appoint Groundmen to pilot all Engines over the single lines leading to and from the Shed at Crockherbtown and Maindy Bridge, under the direction of the respective Signalmen.

● No Engine must foul the single line at either end until the Groundman gives authority for it to do so.

● At Crockherbtown end, the Groundman must be at the Signal Box when not engaged.

● At Maindy Bridge end the Groundman must be at the Engine Sheds end of the line to enable Engines to shunt out and dispose of their vans when required, and he must proceed to Maindy Bridge Signal Box to accompany over the single line incoming Engines upon hearing them whistle for the sheds.

● If the attention of the Groundman at Maindy Bridge cannot be promptly obtained, or he is engaged with another Engine, the Engine requiring to go to the Shed may be sent in by the Crockherbtown entrance.

(Above) Plate 52 - *Taffs Well station looking north with No.5636, a Cathays resident, heading the down C13 mineral train on Thursday, 27th August 1953. The lower photograph, Plate 53, shows the same engine nearly four years later on Saturday, 27th April 1957, still allocated to Cathays but now fitted with a chimney from a 2251 Class 0-6-0. No.5636 is climbing the 1 in 84 gradient towards Penalltau Junction with the C16 8.25am Radyr Junction-Ocean Colliery empties.*

(Above) Plate 54 - Not many depots in the Cardiff Valleys District could boast a tender engine amongst their allocation but between July and September 1957 2-6-0 No.7312 was transferred from Gloucester to Cathays. Sid Rickard was lucky enough to catch the newly arrived engine on the evening of Thursday, 4th July 1957 working tender-first on the Roath Branch with the 7/45pm Radyr Quarry Junction-Severn Tunnel Junction mineral train. In September, No.7312 was transferred to Hereford.

(Below) Plate 55 - No.5670 joins the former Taff Vale Railway main line at Roath Branch Junction with the C12 10.15am Marshalling Sidings-McLaren Colliery empties. Note the unusual signal behind the second wagon with arms for Up and Down trains on the same posts. Friday, 9th April 1954.

Plate 56 - No.5692 approaching St. Fagans on the main line with the return working of the 10.15am Crockherbtown-Briton Ferry Class H freight on Friday, 4th May 1956. The first two wagons in the train, and probably the open wagon to the extreme left of the picture, have been modified to work in conjunction with bolster wagons. In 1941 the GWR modified some 7-plank open wagons for just such a purpose but, regrettably, it is not possible to read the wagon numbers to confirm their origins.

(Above) Plate 57 - Another engine newly transferred to Cathays and caught on film was 2-6-2T No.5574, formerly allocated to Aberbeeg, seen here entering Caerphilly station on the evening of Saturday, 12th May 1956 with the 6/30pm (SO) Cardiff (Queen St.)-Senghenydd auto-train and displaying the 'C AUTO 1' target. The passengers on the adjacent platform are probably off to Cardiff for the evening and will catch the 6/10pm train from Rhymney.

(Below) Plate 58 - Between 1950 and 1953 Cathays had one of the small 16xx 0-6-0PTs on its books, No.1629. It is seen here arriving at Heath Junction on Monday, 27th July 1953 with a breakdown train from the valleys which was subsequently shunted into Heath Low Level Sidings. Note that No.1629 has CP14 chalked on the bunker, indicating that the engine had recently been employed on shunting duties at Salisbury Road, Adam Street and Crwys Sidings. Within a couple of months No.1629 was to be transferred to Worcester, no doubt for use over the tightly restricted lines to the vinegar works.

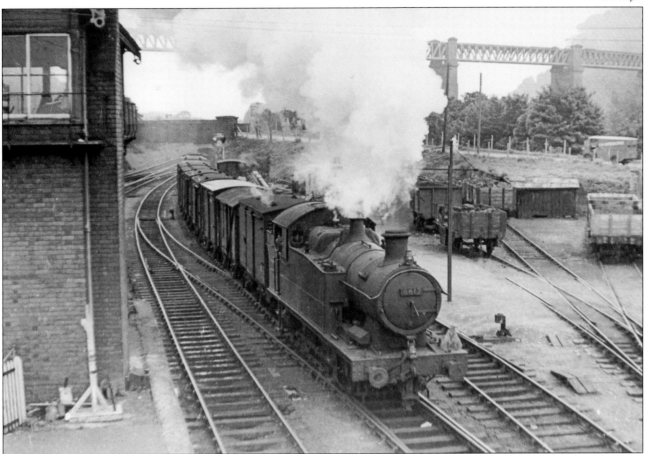

(Above) Plate 59 - On Thursday, 27th August 1953 No.6612 is passing Walnut Tree Junction signal box with the Y14 10.45am Radyr Junction-Dare Valley Junction Class H freight. Although this was a Radyr working the engine was off Cathays shed.

(Below) Plate 60 - The picturesque setting of Pentyrch Crossing, just to the south of Taffs Well and overlooked by Castell Coch, was another location favoured by Sid Rickard. On the afternoon of Saturday, 8th February 1958 No.5669 of Cathays passes by with the C8 12/50pm Llanbradach Colliery-Crwys Sidings mineral train, the engine crew obviously trying to get some protection from the weather by sliding the cab side-sheets back. This locomotive was to be withdrawn from service in September 1964 from Radyr shed and, after a period of time at Woodhams scrapyard on Barry Docks, would pass into preservation.

Plate 61 - Transferred from Treherbert to Cathays the previous month, No.5511 is displaying the 'C AUTO 3' target as it departs from Whitchurch (Glam) propelling the 2/10pm Coryton-Cardiff (Bute Road) service, formed by a pair of ex-Cardiff Railway trailers, on Monday, 16th November 1953.

GABALFA SIDING, MAINDY FUEL.

● Up Line traffic for this Siding must be detached at Cathays and dealt with thence by Pilot. Down traffic must be detached direct, and Drivers of Trains conveying same must whistle for the Down Relief Line from Roath Branch Junction.

UP LINE SIDINGS - ROATH BRANCH JUNCTION.

● The Up Line Sidings are divided into two sections, namely, Lower and Top Sidings. They are under the control of the Shunter.
● No. 6 Top Siding must be kept clear of traffic, in order to give access to the Up Yard from Roath Line South Ground Frame or Roath Branch Junction Signal Box.
● The Signalman at Roath Branch Junction must not divert a train into No.6 Siding until he has ascertained by telephone from the Shunter that the line is clear and that the handpoints are properly set.

DOWN LINE SIDINGS - ROATH BRANCH JUNCTION.

● The back road (No.7 Siding) on the Down side of the line must be kept free as a running line, and no Train or Engine must be allowed to start from either end to proceed to the other without the permission of the person in charge, who must, before giving such permission, satisfy himself by enquiry of the person in charge at the other end that the line is clear for the Engine or Train to proceed.

FRAM WORKS SIDING - ROATH BRANCH JUNCTION.

● 1. This Siding is on the Up Line side between Roath Branch Junction and Llandaff, and has a Junction with the Down Lines at College Road Bridge.
● 2. This is a compound Junction forming a crossover road between the Up and Down Main Lines.
● 3. Traffic from and to this Siding is dealt with as ordered by the Cardiff Queen Street Controller. Loose shunting of vehicles on to this Siding is prohibited.

(Right) Plate 63 - No.5663 is also on the Roath Branch, though working the C25 2/0pm Marshalling Sidings-Ocean Colliery empties, probably in November 1953. This locomotive had been transferred from Treherbert to Cathays during the previous month.

(Above) Plate 62 - Another view of No.5669, this time on the Roath Branch with an Up train of mineral empties on the evening of Tuesday, 25th June 1957. If the C33 target number chalked on the buffer beam is correct, the train is the 6/15pm Roath Branch Junction-Maerdy empties which have started from Marshalling Sidings on this day. The building to the right of the rear of the train is the former Allensbank Engineering Company.

The Roath Branch

(Above) Plate 64 - No.6684, of Cathays, is near Pyle West Junction with the return working of the 10.15am Crockherbtown-Briton Ferry Class H goods on Thursday, 5th January 1956. No doubt the crew will have been busy preparing the engine to tackle the 1 in 93 gradient on the climb from Pyle to Stormy Down.

(Below) Plate 65 - No.5630 passes Penrhos Junction signal box with a Walnut Tree West-Aber Junction Class K freight, part of the Cathays CP4 turn, on Friday, 9th July 1954. From left to right the lines are Up and Down for Cadoxton (via Walnut Tree West and Tynycaeau Junction), Up and Down for Walnut Tree Junction and Up and Down for Pontypridd. The bridge abutments partially visible in the background once carried the former Barry Railway line from Walnut Tree Viaduct to Energlyn, where it joined the Rhymney Railway, and then across the valley to join the Brecon & Merthyr Railway at Barry Junction, crossing the Penyrheol and Llanbradach Viaducts on the way.

Plate 66 - A rather imposing view of No.6647 approaching St. Fagans station with the 10.15am Crockherbtown-Briton Ferry Class H goods on Saturday, 4th April 1953. There was also an evening working on Mondays to Fridays, the 8/0pm Crockherbtown-Briton Ferry, that lured Cathays engines west of Cardiff.

Plate 67 - Former Taff Vale Railway A Class 0-6-2T No.347 (TVR No.75) carrying the Cathays CA target, passing Heath Junction with a Down passenger train from the Rhymney Valley on Saturday, 19th March 1955. Heath (High Level) station can be seen in the background and the Coryton Branch diverging to the left in the foreground.

Taff Vale Railway Class A 0-6-2Ts

Plate 68 - Another former Taff Vale Railway Class A 0-6-2T to be allocated to Cathays was No.307 (TVR No.415 then GWR No.406), seen carrying the CA target and departing from Llanishen Station with a Down passenger train from the Rhymney Valley. Note that the engine still has the original water tanks fitted. Monday, 31st May 1954.

SHUNTING AT LLANISHEN STATION.

● Before shunting is commenced between the Mileage Yard and the Up Line Siding, Points (No.6) south of the Station must be set for the Siding and remain so until the shunting is completed in order to trap any vehicle which may run away. When it is necessary to run the Engine round an Up Train at Llanishen Station for the purpose of returning to Cardiff, the Train must stand on the Up Line while the Engine runs round, and Points No.6 must not be altered for the Main Line until the Engine is ready to cross from Down Line to Up Line.

● Vehicles must not be moved in the right direction on the Down Line at Llanishen Station unless there is an Engine at the Cardiff end of the vehicles.

TRAINS LEFT ON DOWN LOOP LINE BETWEEN HEATH JUNCTION AND CRWYS SIDINGS.

● Guards of Trains arriving on the Down Loop Line between Heath Junction and Crwys must, after the Train has come to a stand, lock up the vans and proceed to the Crwys Shunters' Cabin, unless instructions are received to the contrary.

FAIR OAK SIDING.

● Fair Oak Siding is situated between Crwys Siding and Heath Junction Boxes, near Crwys Box Down Distant Signal, and is connected with the Up Line only. The Up Line is on a gradient of 1 in 80, falling towards Crwys Sidings. The connection is worked by a two-lever Ground Frame which is locked by an Annetts Key. The Annetts Key is kept in the locking frame at Crwys Box, attached to lever No.20 working the Up Line Starting Signal. The withdrawal of the Annetts Key from the locking frame locks the Up Starting Signal Lever at Danger.

● Trains going to Fair Oak Siding must always have a Brake Van at the rear in which the Guard must ride. The Brake Van must always be the leading vehicle when the Train returns to Crwys Siding. After sunset a red light must be carried at the leading end of the Brake Van when returning from Fair Oak Siding.

Plate 69 - On Saturday, 9th April 1955, No.4580 from Cathays passes Cherry Orchard signal box with Up empty coaching stock for an auto-train working, probably a Senghenydd to Cardiff service. The engine is displaying the 'C AUTO 3' target and was photographed from the lofty footbridge on the south end of Cefn On Halt.

(Right) Plate 72 - On Friday, 3rd September 1954, former Taff Vale Railway Class A 0-6-2T No.360 (TVR No.125), carrying the Cathays CC target, passes Cherry Orchard Sidings with the 11.44am Rhymney-Cardiff (Bute Road) passenger train as former Rhymney Railway Class A1 0-6-2T No.66 (RR No.26) shunts the 11.15am goods from Penrhos Junction.

(Left) Plate 70 - Having just passed under the Wedal Road bridge, No.6635 of Cathays appears to be working hard with the C25 2/0pm Marshalling Sidings-Ocean Colliery empties on Thursday, 14th April 1955. This train would take over two hours to cover the fifteen miles to Penalltau Junction.

(Below) Plate 71 - A Cardiff-Senghenydd auto-train arriving at Cefn On Halt behind another 2-6-2T from Cathays shed, No.4589. The train is under the footbridge from which the photograph of No.4580 was taken in Plate 69. Thursday, 11th August 1955.

CHERRY ORCHARD SIDINGS.

● The Reception Sidings at Cherry Orchard numbered 1 to 4 are accessible at both ends. The points and signals leading to the Sidings are connected to, and worked from, Cherry Orchard Signal Box.

● As far as practicable, No.1 Siding, next to the Down Goods Loop, must be kept clear for the reception of Up trains, and No.4 Siding for Down trains. Before lowering the Signals for a train to enter the Reception Sidings, the Signalman must have an assurance from the Cefn-On Guard that the hand points, over which the train will have to travel are properly set and that the Siding is clear. An Up train must not be allowed to run into the Sidings if a Down Freight train is in the Section until such train has passed, or has been brought to a stand at the Down Home Signal, or the Down Goods Loop Starting Signal, as the case may be. Under no circumstances must an Up train be propelled from the Reception Sidings to the Up Main Line unless the Guard is riding in the Brake Van.

● Drivers of Up and Down trains entering the Reception Sidings must keep a sharp look out, and be prepared to stop clear of any obstruction.

● Down Through Freight trains must travel over the Down Goods Loop, and the Signalman must keep the points for that line set for the Sand Drag Siding until the approaching train has been brought to a stand at the Stop Board. The Guards of Down Freight trains stopped at the Stop Board must go forward to assist the Bank Guard to apply brakes and when the Bank Guard is not available for this work, the Guard himself must secure the necessary brakes.

● The group of Sidings adjacent to the Carriage Shed are numbered 1 to 8, and are normally used for storage purposes. As far as practicable, No.1 Siding, next to the Carriage Shed, must be kept clear and the hand points set for that line. At the South end of the Sidings a Single Lever Ground Frame is provided for working the points leading from No.1 Siding to the Shunting Spur. The points are secured in the normal position for the Shunting Spur by a chain and padlock, the key of which is kept in Cherry Orchard Signal Box.

● One of the Sidings in the Carriage Shed has been extended at the South end to connect with No.1 Siding to enable traffic to be berthed or picked up at that end.

VICTORIA COAL SIDING - CRWYS.

● Victoria Siding is situated on the Down Side of the line near Crwys Road, and is connected with the Down Goods Running Loop only. The points are worked by a single lever Ground Frame which is normally padlocked for Trains to pass down the Down Goods Loop. The key of the padlock must be kept in Crwys Signal Box. The Guard or Shunter requiring to work in Victoria Siding must obtain the key from the Signalman and when the work at the Siding is completed he must padlock the Ground Frame lever and return the key to the Signalman.

● While shunting is being performed at Victoria Siding no Train or Engine must be allowed to pass through the crossover road between the Down Goods Loop and Down Main Line.

Plate 73 - The 10.44am Rhymney-Cardiff (General) passenger train approaches Ystrad Mynach station behind No.4129 on Monday, 7th September 1957. The 1 in 145/106 rising gradient towards Hengoed can be seen in the background as the line curves away to the right.

Locomotives allocated to Cathays during 1957 included:

0-6-2T Nos.305, 381, 383, 385, 390
0-6-0PT Nos.3672, 3727
2-6-2T Nos.4101, 4122, 4123, 4124, 4126, 4129, 4177
2-6-2T Nos.4553, 4580, 4589
0-6-0PT Nos.4618, 4634, 4667, 4672, 4698
2-6-2T Nos.5511, 5534, 5545, 5568, 5572, 5574
0-6-2T Nos.5601, 5622, 5627, 5630, 5636, 5653, 5654, 5663, 5669, 5670, 5683, 5687, 5692
0-6-0PT Nos.5710, 5724, 5727, 5793
0-6-0PT Nos.6402, 6416, 6434, 6435
0-6-2T Nos.6603, 6606, 6607, 6608, 6612, 6614, 6618, 6624, 6626, 6633, 6635, 6638, 6647, 6648, 6659, 6660, 6665, 6682, 6684, 6689
2-8-2T Nos.7202, 7205, 7242
2-6-0 No.7312
0-6-0PT No.7445
0-6-0PT Nos.7722, 7726, 7738, 7751, 7772, 7779
0-6-0PT Nos.8469, 8470, 8471, 8478, 8481, 8482, 8484, 8489
0-6-0PT No.8780
0-6-0PT Nos.9679, 9769, 9776

(Above) Plate 74 - A lunchtime Caerphilly-Cardiff passenger train leaving Llanishen station behind No.6682 on Thursday, 10th January 1957. No.6682 was a Cathays engine for quite a few years and stayed in the Cardiff area until being withdrawn from Radyr shed in February 1964.

(Below) Plate 75 - Ex-Taff Vale Railway Class A 0-6-2T No.364 (TVR No.129) leaves Heath Junction with the 1/46pm Coryton-Cardiff (Bute Road) passenger train. It is about to pass former Rhymney Railway Class R 0-6-2T No.35 (RR No.39) working the afternoon D8 Cardiff Docks-Llanbradach Colliery freight which has been brought down to walking pace, the driver anticipating that he will be given the road once No.364 has cleared the junction. Friday, 7th November 1952.

88A *RADYR JUNCTION*

Prior to December 1957 Radyr was an uncoded sub-shed of Cardiff (Cathays). During that month, however, Radyr was allocated the code 88A after the transfer of the majority of locomotives from Cathays. Renumbered 88B on 1st January 1961, Radyr was to close to steam in July 1965. The shed, a four road dead-end building, was opened by the GWR on 29th September 1931, replacing the former Taff Vale Railway two road shed at the south end of Radyr Station.

In the winter of 1957/58, the shed was responsible for the working of 25 mineral and freight turns, described below.

Target No.	Start time; time off shed	Start point, destination and notes + - Runs if required
Y1	**4.10am MX** Off shed 3.55am;	Work Radyr Junction to Treherbert
+Y1	**5.25am MO** Off shed 5.15am;	Work Radyr Quarry Junction as ordered by Control
Y2	**2.30am MX** Off shed 2.10am;	Work Radyr Junction to Merthyr
Y3	**4.20am** Off shed 4.15am;	Work Radyr Junction to Aber Junction - Shunting; 3 turns SX, 2 turns SO
Y5	**7.20am** Off shed 7.10am;	Work Radyr Quarry Junction to Pengam Sidings
Y6	**6.30am** Off shed 6.20am;	Work Radyr Quarry Junction to Grangetown
Y7	**5.20am** Off shed 5.5am;	Work Radyr Junction to Maerdy Colliery
Y8	**9.25am** Off shed 9.10am;	Work Radyr Quarry Junction to Severn Tunnel Junction
Y9	**6.15am** Off shed 6.10am;	Work Radyr Junction Van Siding to Aber Junction and Wernddu
Y10	**6.50am** Off shed 6.35am;	Work Radyr Quarry Junction to Roath Basin Jct and Creigiau Quarries; 16 hrs
Y11	**8.20am** Off shed 8.0am;	Work Radyr Quarry Junction to Roath Branch
+Y12	**7.05am** Off shed 6.45am;	Work Radyr Junction as ordered by Control
Y13	**4.20am** Off shed 4.15am;	Work Radyr Junction Van Siding to Windsor Colliery
Y14	**10.45am** Off shed 10.30am;	Work Radyr Junction to Dare Valley Junction
Y15	**10.25am** Off shed 10.10am;	Work Radyr Junction to Treherbert Junction
Y23	**12/05pm** Off shed 12noon;	Work Radyr Junction Van Siding to Windsor Colliery
Y24	**1/45pm** Off shed 1/30pm;	Work Radyr Quarry Junction to Roath Power Station and Nantgarw Colliery
Y25	**3/05pm** Off shed 2/45pm;	Work Radyr Junction to Cwm Colliery
+Y26	**11.50am** Off shed 11.40am;	Work Radyr Junction Van Siding to Pentyrch and Rockwood Colliery
Y27	**4/25pm SX** Off shed 4/20pm; **1/30pm SO** Off shed 1/15pm;	Work Radyr Junction to Pontypridd and Cardiff (Newtown)
Y29	**10/25pm SX** Off shed 10/20pm; **7/0pm SO** Off shed 6/55pm;	Work Radyr Junction Van Siding to Aber Junction; shunting
+Y33	**10/20pm** Off shed 10/15pm;	Work Radyr Quarry Junction as required

There were further workings, but without Target numbers, from Radyr Quarry Junction to Severn Tunnel Junction at: **1.0am (MX)** (Off shed 12.45am); **1/15pm** (Off shed 1/0pm) and **7/45pm** (Off shed 7/0pm). Finally, there was a **2.35am MX** (Off shed 2.15am) **5.45am MO** (Off shed 5.30am) Radyr Quarry Junction to Salisbury.

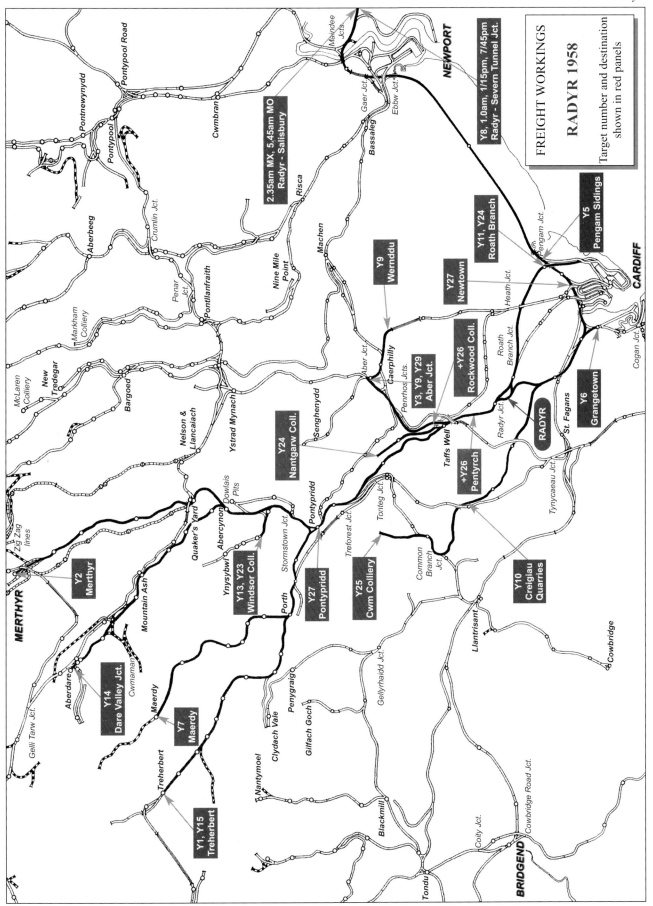

FREIGHT WORKINGS

RADYR 1958

Target number and destination shown in red panels

Y8, 1.0am, 1/15pm, 7/45pm Radyr - Severn Tunnel Jct.

2.35am MX, 5.45am MO Radyr - Salisbury

Y9 Wernddu

Y11, Y24 Roath Branch

Y5 Pengam Sidings

Y27 Newtown

+Y26 Rockwood Coll.

Y3, Y9, Y29 Aber Jct.

Y6 Grangetown

+Y26 Pentyrch

RADYR

Y24 Nantgarw Coll.

Y2 Merthyr

Y13, Y23 Windsor Coll.

Y27 Pontypridd

Y25 Cwm Colliery

Y10 Creigiau Quarries

Y14 Dare Valley Jct.

Y7 Maerdy

Y1, Y15 Treherbert

NEWPORT

CARDIFF

MERTHYR

BRIDGEND

Locomotives allocated to Radyr during 1957 included:

0-6-0PT Nos.3400, 3401, 3402, 3403, 3404, 3405, 3406
0-6-0PT Nos.3672, 3727
2-6-2T Nos.4101, 4122, 4123, 4124, 4126, 4129, 4177
2-6-2T No.4580
0-6-0PT Nos.4618, 4634, 4667, 4672, 4698
2-6-2T Nos.5534, 5568, 5572, 5574
0-6-2T Nos.5622, 5636, 5669, 5670, 5683, 5692
0-6-0PT No.5793
0-6-0PT Nos.6402, 6434
0-6-2T Nos.6603, 6606, 6607, 6608, 6612, 6614, 6618, 6624, 6626, 6633, 6638, 6647, 6648, 6659, 6660, 6665, 6682, 6684, 6689
2-8-2T Nos.7202, 7205, 7242
0-6-0PT Nos.7726, 7738, 7751, 7772, 7779
0-6-0PT Nos.8469, 8470, 8471, 8478, 8481, 8482, 8484, 8489
0-6-0PT No.8780
0-6-0PT Nos.9679, 9776

WORKING OF ENGINES TO AND FROM RADYR ENGINE SHED.

● Engines working to and from Shed at Radyr Junction must run over the Inlet and Outlet Roads respectively between the Ground Frame and the entrance to the Shed Sidings. The Inlet Road must be kept clear and Engines going to Shed must not stand on that line longer than is necessary. There is an outlet from the Shed at Radyr Quarry, and engines must not be taken past the Stopboard until permission has been obtained from the Yard Foreman or Shunter.

Plate 76 - On Wednesday, 11th March 1959, No.6612, of Radyr shed was routed over the Down Relief line at Gaer Junction, Newport, with a westbound Class H goods, which is probably a return working of one of the Radyr Quarry Junction-Severn Tunnel Junction turns. Note the AWS ramps between the rails of the Up and Down main lines in the foreground.

Plate 77 - Radyr had several 41xx 2-6-2Ts allocated and amongst them was No.4160 seen leaving Bridgend station with the 2Z30 9.30am Rhymney-Porthcawl excursion on Saturday, 7th July 1962. The excursion was for parties from Rhymney and Pontlottyn Sunday Schools and Van Road Sunday School, a total of 450 passengers in five carriages. After withdrawal in June 1965 the engine spent the next nine years in Woodhams scrapyard on Barry Docks before passing into preservation.

(Above) Plate 78 - No.4163 had by now been reallocated from Barry to Radyr and is seen here passing Maesmawr with the Z55 seven coach excursion from the Rhondda Valley to Barry Island on Monday, 1st August 1960. The signal above the last coach of the train indicates the course of the line from Treforest Junction to Tonteg Junction.

(Below) Plate 79 - Nearing the end of its days, a very begrimed No.4166 from Radyr shed heads the Up H14 freight along the Roath Branch on Saturday, 17th August 1963. This photograph was taken during one of Sid's visits to South Wales and it was only four years since he had photographed the same engine at Weymouth and looking in much better condition.

Plate 80 - Radyr's No.6608 approaches Heath Junction with the C8 9.22am Crwys Sidings-Llanbradach Colliery empties on Friday, 15th May 1959. The signalman has also set the road for the 8.24am Rhymney-Cardiff passenger train.

Plate 81 - No.4177 seemed to be a favourite with the Radyr shed staff who invariably kept the engine in a clean condition as this view testifies. No.4177 is leaving Coryton Halt with a seven-coach excursion for Porthcawl, reporting number 35, on Thursday, 29th May 1958.

Plate 82 - No.5684 near Birchgrove Halt with a Cardiff-Coryton passenger train on Saturday, 1st February 1958. This locomotive had been transferred from Oxley to Radyr the previous month but it stayed only until the following June when it was again transferred, this time to Treherbert.

DOWN FREIGHT TRAINS CALLING AT RADYR JUNCTION.

● To facilitate the breaking up of trains at Radyr Junction, Down Freight trains on arrival at that point must, as far as possible, be formed as follows:- Engine, Class 3 traffic, Other traffic.

● The Shunting Engines at the various Goods Yards must form wagons for Radyr Junction and beyond in this order, so that the train engines may, by keeping the Class 3 traffic attached to the engine, pick up in one shunt at each place.

● Down Freight Trains calling at Radyr Junction, and arriving on the Main Line, must be drawn clear into the Yard, and trains for Cardiff must pass out of the Yard via Llandaff Loop.

● Mixed load trains arriving on the Down Relief Line may be divided outside the junction or drawn into the Yard, according to the circumstances.

● The target number of each Down Freight Train will be advised to the Radyr Junction Signalman from Pentyrch Crossing Box, and Instructions must be obtained from the Yard Inspector's Office as to how the train shall be dealt with.

Plate 83 - Heath Low Level, Saturday, 31st October 1953.

CARDIFF RAILWAY COMPANY
BEWARE OF TRAINS
PERSONS TRESPASSING ALONG THE RAILWAY OR ON THE COMPANY'S PROPERTY WILL BE PROSECUTED.
BY ORDER

(Above) Plate 84 - No.5692, by this time allocated to Radyr shed, sports an express headcode near Treforest with a ten-coach train of empty corridor stock on Monday, 1st August 1960. These carriages were to be used on a subsequent Cardiff valleys to Paddington excursion that was routed via Caerphilly, Machen and Newport. On the occasions that Sid managed to photograph these trains on their outward journey over the PC&N, they were hauled by double-headed 56xx Class 0-6-2Ts or 41xx Class 2-6-2Ts.

(Below) Plate 85 - Radyr's No.5635 passes Cherry Orchard Wagon Works with the H33 2/25pm Marshalling Sidings-Ogilvie Colliery empties on Monday, 19th August 1963. Like most steam engines during this period No.5635, although apparently steam tight, looks to be in a very dirty condition.

Plate 86 - Pentyrch Crossing looking south towards Radyr with 56xx Class 0-6-2T No.5687 heading the C29 2/55pm Marshalling Sidings-Ogilvie Colliery empties.

Pentyrch Crossing on Saturday, 8th February 1958

Plate 87 - The view up the line; No.4618 had been reallocated from Cathays to Radyr during the previous month and was caught on film near Pentyrch Crossing with a Cardiff (East Dock) working, the D10, which was the Nantgarw Colliery-Cardiff Docks goods; quite a light load on this day.

Plate 88 - Former Great Western Railway signals at Roath Branch Junction on Saturday, 19th May 1956.

(Below) Plate 89 - No.6614 from Radyr shed passes Heath Junction and heads towards the coalfields with the H21 1/12pm Crwys Sidings-Groesfaen Colliery empties on Monday, 6th April 1964, another occasion when Sid revisited South Wales. Track rationalisation is underway with the lifting of the Down Relief line and the siding in the foreground.

Plate 90 - A bird's eye view of Pontypridd station and junction on Tuesday, 12th June 1956. A 56xx Class 0-6-2T is at the station with the 1/0pm Barry Island-Merthyr passenger train, which will branch off to the right at the junction. Another 56xx 0-6-2T can be seen heading up the Rhondda Valley with a train of mineral empties.

(Above) Plate 91 - Another 56xx Class 0-6-2T allocated to Radyr was No.5669, here crossing the causeway between Barry Island and Barry Town with an Up passenger train on Wednesday, 6th August 1958. During the following month the locomotive was transferred to Treherbert for a short time before returning to Radyr. Note the former Barry Railway somersault signal complete with elegant finial, also the Bristol Lodeka bus of the Western Welsh Omnibus Co. Ltd.
Having been withdrawn from service from Radyr shed in September 1964, No.5669 spent a long period at Woodhams scrapyard on Barry Docks before passing into preservation. How much would the registration number on the Morris car be worth today?

(Below) Plate 92 - Radyr's No.6606 passing Fontigary, west of Rhoose, with a passenger train for Bridgend on Friday, 10th June 1960.

(Above) Plate 93 - Approaching Beddau Loop Junction on Saturday, 16th February 1957 was 0-6-0PT No.7726 of Radyr with a Down mineral train for Radyr Yard. It is unknown what the working is, as the Y6 target carried by the engine denotes it as working between Radyr Quarry Junction and Grangetown during this period.

(Below) Plate 94 - No.6608 from Radyr shed draws into Cardiff (Queen St.) station with a Down train of empty coaching stock on Saturday, 31st January 1959. Judging by the amount of coal in the bunker, this is No.6608's first duty of the day.

(Above) Plate 95 - No.4129 spent from January 1958 until February 1959 allocated to Radyr shed. On Wednesday, 6th August 1958 No.4129 waits to draw into Barry Island station with stock for a return excursion to the Cardiff valleys. To the left of the picture stands the short-lived DMU servicing point.

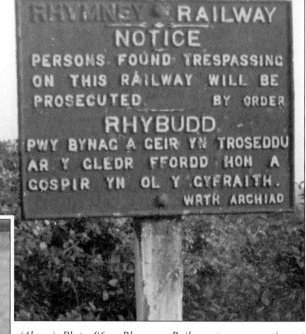

RHYMNEY RAILWAY NOTICE
PERSONS FOUND TRESPASSING ON THIS RAILWAY WILL BE PROSECUTED. BY ORDER

RHYBUDD
PWY BYNAG A GEIR YN TROSEDDU AR Y GLEDR FFORDD HON A GOSPIR YN OL Y GYFRAITH.
WRTH ARCHIAD

BARRY DOCK AND RAILWAYS TRESPASS NOTICE
ALL PERSONS ARE WARNED NOT TO TRESPASS UPON THE DOCK PROPERTY, RAILWAYS OR STATIONS OF THE COMPANY. AND NOTICE IS HEREBY GIVEN PURSUANT TO THE PROVISIONS OF THE COMPANY'S ACTS EVERY PERSON WHO TRESPASSES UPON ANY SUCH DOCK PROPERTY, RAILWAYS OR STATIONS IN SUCH MANNER AS TO EXPOSE HIMSELF TO DANGER OR RISK OF DANGER RENDERS HIMSELF LIABLE TO A PENALTY NOT EXCEEDING FORTY SHILLINGS AND IN DEFAULT OF PAYMENT TO ONE MONTHS IMPRISONMENT FOR EVERY SUCH OFFENCE.

(Above) Plate 96 - Rhymney Railway trespass notice at Heath Junction; Wednesday, 23rd September 1953.

You have
been warned ....

(Left) Plate 97 - A more verbose example from the Barry Railway at Tonteg Junction; Thursday, 25th October 1956.

Plate 98 - Radyr's No.6684 puts in an unexpected appearance at Heath Junction when working a Down passenger train from the Rhymney Valley on Wednesday, 30th April 1958. The engine had been employed on shunting duties at Caerphilly when the train engine of this passenger train had failed, necessitating the use of No.6684 to complete the journey. The CP9 target is testimony to the locomotive's previous employment.

88B   *CARDIFF EAST DOCK*

Cardiff East Dock shed was coded 88B. An eight-road dead-end shed, it was built by the GWR and opened in 1931, replacing the former Rhymney Railway shed on the same site. East Dock closed to steam on 8th March 1958 and lost its code from 1st January 1961 but, when Canton closed to steam on 9th September 1962, steam was restored to East Dock. The shed had been designated 88L on 24th February 1962 but subsequently changed to 88A on 9th September 1963. It was the last steam shed in use in the area, closing on the 2nd August 1965.

In the winter of 1957/58, the shed was responsible for the working of 10 mineral and freight turns, described below.

D1	**3.40am** Off shed 3.30am;	Work Roath Basin Junction to Rhymney
D2	**4.15am** Off shed 4.5am;	Work Roath Basin Junction to Cwm Bargoed
D3	**4.30am** Off shed 4.20am;	Work Roath Basin Junction to Ystrad Mynach (16 hours)
D4	**7.50am** Off shed 7.40am;	Work Roath Basin Junction to Hengoed Junction
D5	**5.0am** Off shed 4.50am;	Work Roath Basin Junction to Whitchurch
D6	**7.15am** Off shed 7.5am;	Work Roath Basin Junction to Nantgarw Colliery (MO); Cherry Orchard thence Penrhos Junction (MX)
D7	**10.5am** Off shed 9.55am;	Work Roath Basin Junction to Bargoed Pits
D8	**1/55pm SX** Off shed 1/45pm;	Work Roath Basin Junction to Llanbradach
D9	**11.15am SX** Off shed 11.5am; **9.45am SO** Off shed 9.35am;	Work Roath Basin Junction to Cherry Orchard
D10	**8.30am** Off shed 8.20am;	Work Roath Basin Junction to Nantgarw Colliery

ENGINES GOING TO EAST DOCK ENGINE SHED.
● A telephone is provided at the entrance to East Dock Engine Shed, and the Fireman of an engine which has come through the section from Tyndall Street Junction will be responsible for advising the Signalman at Stonefield Signal Box by telephone whether or not the engine has arrived clear of the running line with tail lamp attached.

FREIGHT TRAIN TERMINATING AT ROATH BASIN JUNCTION YARD.
● A telephone is provided on the Down Line Inner Home Signal, and the Guard of a Freight Train which has come through the section from Tyndall Street Junction will be responsible for advising the Signalman at Stonefield Signal Box by telephone whether or not the train has arrived clear of the running line, complete with tail lamp.

Locomotives allocated to Cardiff East Dock during 1957 included:

0-6-2T Nos.36, 38, 42, 43
0-6-0PT Nos.3400, 3401, 3402, 3403, 3404, 3405, 3406, 3407, 3408, 3409
0-6-0PT Nos.3681, 3694, 3730, 3734, 3783
0-6-0PT Nos.4626, 4631, 4686, 4698
0-6-2T Nos.5648, 5666, 5687
0-6-0PT Nos.6700, 6701, 6702, 6703, 6704, 6705, 6706, 6707, 6708, 6709, 6744, 6751, 6765, 6767, 6769, 6770, 6771, 6773, 6774, 6775, 6778
0-6-0PT Nos.7722, 7738
0-6-0PT Nos.8414, 8416, 8424, 8429, 8437, 8438, 8441, 8457, 8464
0-6-0PT Nos.8722, 8743, 8787
0-6-0PT Nos.9437, 9443, 9477
0-6-0PT Nos.9677, 9679, 9769, 9776

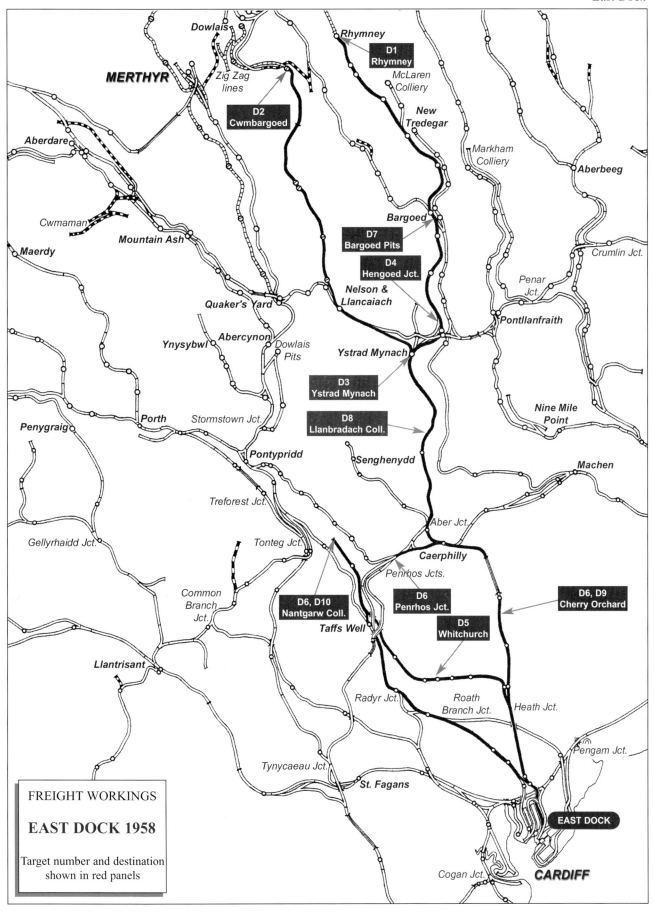

Dowlais

MERTHYR

Zig Zag
lines

D2
Cwmbargoed

Aberdare

Cwmaman

Maerdy

Mountain Ash

Quaker's Yard

Ynysybwl   Abercynon

Penygraig

Dowlais
Pits

Porth   Stormstown Jct.

Pontypridd

Treforest Jct.

Gellyrhaidd Jct.   Tonteg Jct.

Common
Branch
Jct.

D6, D10
Nantgarw Coll.

Llantrisant

Taffs Well

Radyr Jct.

Tynycaeau Jct.

St. Fagans

Cogan Jct.

Rhymney

D1
Rhymney

McLaren
Colliery

*New
Tredegar*

Markham
Colliery

Aberbeeg

Bargoed

D7
Bargoed Pits

D4
Hengoed Jct.

Crumlin Jct.

Nelson &
Llancaiach

Penar
Jct.

Pontllanfraith

Ystrad Mynach

D3
Ystrad Mynach

Nine Mile
Point

D8
Llanbradach Coll.

Senghenydd

Machen

Aber Jct.

Caerphilly

Penrhos Jcts.

D6
Penrhos Jct.

D6, D9
Cherry Orchard

D5
Whitchurch

Roath
Branch Jct.   Heath Jct.

Pengam Jct.

EAST DOCK

CARDIFF

FREIGHT WORKINGS

EAST DOCK 1958

Target number and destination
shown in red panels

Plate 99 - Former Rhymney Railway Class P 0-6-2T No.83 (RR No.6) climbing towards Heath (High Level) station with the D8 Roath Basin Junction-Llanbradach Colliery empties on Friday,14th January 1955, just four months before withdrawal. The locomotive had been transferred to Cardiff East Dock from Rhymney in October 1953.

WATER FOR ENGINES WORKING BETWEEN CARDIFF DOCKS AND CRWYS.

Engines working to and from the Docks are to take water as follows:-

● Engines from Docks to Crwys Sidings to take water on the Up journey at Machine Road, Crwys. This should enable the Engine to work to the Docks and back again without taking fresh supplies.

● Engines from Docks to the Heath or Llanishen Sidings to take water at Crwys before forming their Trains for the Down trip.

● Under no circumstances are Drivers working from Crwys to the Docks to take water at Gaol Lane Sidings or Cardiff Docks Shed (R.R.).

Plate 100 - Former Rhymney Railway Class R 0-6-2T No.38 (RR No.42) on the Roath Branch with the D10 Nantgarw Colliery-Cardiff Docks mineral train on Saturday, 26th January 1957. This locomotive would be withdrawn from East Dock shed in the following October.

Plate 101 - 0-6-0PT No.8464, of Cardiff East Dock shed, passes Llanishen station and goods yard with the D9 Roath Basin Junction–Cherry Orchard freight some time in 1957. Note the small ground frame for operating the goods yard on the right of the picture, just the other side of the bridge.

Plate 102 - The southern portal of Caerphilly Tunnel seen from Cefn On Halt c.1956. Caerphilly Tunnel was one of those in the South Wales district where trains had to have a tail-light lit during daylight hours. Interestingly, the Sectional Appendix for the period describes the operation of a Clapper in the tunnel, details of which are in the panel below. Note the white quadrant on the Up Home signal; this was fitted as an aid to sighting the signal arm.

WORKING OF DOWN FREIGHT TRAINS THROUGH CAERPHILLY TUNNEL TO LLANISHEN.

● As far as possible the outside brakes must be used at Tunnel North, and those on the six-foot side at Tunnel South.

● All Down Freight Trains must enter the Tunnel at a speed not exceeding four miles an hour, and the speed must not be increased until the whole of the Train is in the Tunnel.

● A Clapper is fixed on the Down Line in Caerphilly Tunnel about 303 yards from the South end, to indicate to Drivers that the Train is approaching the mouth of the Tunnel. It is operated by a treadle, and every pair of wheels will sound the Clapper.

Should the Driver notice any defect in the working of the Clapper, it must be specially reported at the next stopping place, so that it can be attended to as quickly as possible.

● Drivers of all Up Trains must sound the Engine whistles in accordance with Rule 127 (vi), when approaching the North end of the Caerphilly Tunnel, to give warning to the Guards at that place.

ENGINE ASSISTING TRAINS THROUGH CAERPHILLY TUNNEL.

● The Driver of the Assisting Engine must give a crow whistle on passing Cherry Orchard to indicate to the Signalman that the Engine will go through the Tunnel.

CAERPHILLY TUNNEL - WAGONS WITH BROKEN COUPLINGS.

● When the couplings of wagons from points North of Caerphilly Tunnel to Cardiff are found to be broken, the wagons must not be conveyed through the Tunnel, but must be put off at Aber Junction or Wernddu for repairs.

(Right) Plate 104 - Another view of former Rhymney Railway Class R 0-6-2T No.38 (RR No.42), this time at Ystrad Mynach with a train of mineral empties from Cardiff Docks on Saturday, 7th September 1957.

(Above) Plate 103 - Drawing into Cherry Orchard Sidings is another of the former Rhymney Railway Class R 0-6-2Ts allocated to Cardiff East Dock shed, No.40 (RR No.36), working the D2 Cwm Bargoed-Cardiff Docks freight on Tuesday, 12th August 1952. It was only in the October of 1949 that No.40 had been rebuilt with a Great Western style taper boiler at Caerphilly Works, but even in this form the engine only lasted until October 1953 before being withdrawn.

Plate 105 - Former Rhymney Railway Class R 0-6-2T No.36 (RR No.40) rounding the curve at Beddau Loop Junction with the D2 Cwm Bargoed-Cardiff Docks goods on Saturday, 16th February 1957, eight months before withdrawal. Note the slag ladles in the train consist; they have been turned on their sides to give better stability.

TRAINS WITH ASSISTING ENGINE IN REAR, CRWYS SIDINGS TO CHERRY ORCHARD.

● These Trains must not consist of more than 76 wagons in addition to the two Engines and Brake Van. The Yard Foreman at Stonefield Junction must advise the Crwys Yard Shunter what Trains are to be assisted and the latter must arrange accordingly.

● The following margins must be maintained in front of Passenger Trains:-

	Crwys.	Heath Junction and Llanishen.
Single Trains	7 minutes	.. 4 minutes
Double Trains	9	.. 5

● The running times must not exceed the following:-

	Crwys to Cherry Orchard.
Single Trains	15 minutes
Double Trains	20

● Drivers of Assisting Engines must shut off steam in time to leave the Train at Cherry Orchard Signal Box, but must not reverse until a "Right Away" Signal is received from the Train Guard. The Guard must satisfy himself that the Train is in order before giving this signal to the Drivers of assisting engines who, if called forward by the Guard, must hold the rear part of the Train in case a parting occurs.

SHUNTING AT CHERRY ORCHARD and CRWYS SIDINGS.

Cardiff East Dock duties included carrying out shunting at Cherry Orchard and Crwys Sidings. Duty D5, nominally working to Whitchurch, included 2½ hours (Monday to Saturday) shunting at Crwys Sidings.

Two East Dock engines shunted Cherry Orchard Wagon Repair Shops; D9 for 5¼ hours (Monday to Friday) from 12 noon (half an hour less on Saturdays), by which time D6 had already completed its stint between 8am and 10am (Tuesdays to Saturdays) after which it worked to Penrhos Junction.

Plate 106 - Watford Crossing, Caerphilly, under a snow-laden sky on Saturday, 16th February 1957 with another of the former Rhymney Railway Class R 0-6-2Ts from Cardiff East Dock No.42 (RR No.46) passing with the D7 Roath Basin Junction-Bargoed Pits working. This must have been a fairly good day for Sid as he also managed to catch another of the class, No.36, on film as well, even at this late date. No.42 was withdrawn in September 1957.

(Above) Plate 107 - Duty D7 passing Cefn On Halt behind former Rhymney Railway Class R 0-6-2T No.37 (RR No.41) of Cardiff East Dock on Tuesday, 12th August 1952. This locomotive was withdrawn from service in September 1956 and cut up at Barry Works in the following December.

(Below) Plate 108 - Former Rhymney Railway Class A1 0-6-2T No.65 (RR No.25) passes through Cardiff General station with a westbound transfer freight on Friday, 2nd October 1953, two months prior to withdrawal. This East Dock engine had been rebuilt by the GWR with a round-top boiler from a Class A engine thus re-classifying her as Class A, a bit of a retrograde step at the time. In 1931, however, a Standard No.10 boiler was fitted.

Plate 109 - The impressive bulk of the Rhymney Railway Class R 0-6-2Ts is evident in this view of No.36 (RR No.40) on Monday, 31st May 1954, near Llanishen working the D8 duty, Roath Basin Junction-Llanbradach Colliery empties.

Rhymney Railway Class R still at work

Plate 110 - Taffs Well station with former Rhymney Railway Class R 0-6-2T No.41 (RR No. 45) passing through with the D10 Nantgarw Colliery-Cardiff Docks duty on Thursday, 27th August 1953. Cardiff East Dock shed was the last stronghold of former Rhymney Railway engines in the South Wales area with quite a few examples being reallocated to the depot to see out their final years.

(Above) Plate 111 - It was not only former Rhymney Railway engines that were allocated to Cardiff East Dock. 0-6-2T No.155 (CR No.35), the sole surviving 0-6-2T of Cardiff Railway ancestry then in BR use, was another of its engines. Employed here on pilot duties at Pengam on Friday, 13th February 1953, No.155 seems to be putting some effort into the task. This locomotive was withdrawn the following September.
(Below) Plate 112 - A bird's eye view of a Class R 0-6-2T passing the former Cardiff Railway station at Glan-y-Llyn with the D10 Roath Branch Junction-Nantgarw Colliery empties c.1953; possibly Saturday, 4th April.

Plate 113 - A delightful study of a somewhat work-stained ex-Rhymney Railway Class R 0-6-2T No.43 (RR No.47) passing through Cefn On Halt with the D2 Cwm Bargoed-Cardiff Docks freight on Saturday, 31st March 1956. Note the slag ladle towards the rear of the train and also the effectiveness of the sighting board on the Up Home signal. No.43 had been transferred to East Dock from Cathays the previous August and would stay there until withdrawal the following February.

(Above) Plate 114 - 0-6-0PT No.3402 approaches Heath Junction with the D9 Roath Basin Junction-Cherry Orchard Works freight on Saturday, 28th July 1956. At this time the engine was a mere eight months old and, like all other members of this class, had been allocated from new to Cardiff East Dock. Since they were of such a late build, none of the class saw many years' service before being withdrawn.
(Below) Plate 115 - Former Taff Vale Railway Class O4 0-6-2T No.279 (TVR No.2) had recently been transferred to Cardiff East Dock from Abercynon and is employed here on shunting duties at Pengam on Sunday, 24th January 1954, four months prior to withdrawal. Other engines on pilot duties at Pengam on this day included Nos.215 and 8429.

Plate 116 - This is the kind of photograph for which Sid Rickard was renowned, where the railway blended into the industrial scene and landscape. No.5687 had been reallocated from Cathays to Cardiff East Dock earlier this month and is here passing Llanbradach Colliery with the D2 8.45am Cwm Bargoed-Stonefield Junction freight on Saturday, 27th April 1957. Behind No.5687 an Austerity type 0-6-0ST shunts wagons on the cramped internal railway system of Llanbradach Colliery.

(Above) Plate 117 - Now just over a year old and with an 88B shed plate clearly visible, 0-6-0PT No.3400 is pictured near Lake Road East on the Roath Branch with the D10 Roath Basin Junction-Nantgarw Colliery empties on Saturday, 2nd February 1957. The following December would see No.3400 reallocated to Radyr with other engines of the class. It stayed there until October 1958 when it was transferred to Shrewsbury for just over three years but returned to Radyr in May 1962 to rejoin its sister engines.

(Below) Plate 118 - 0-6-0PT No.8429 of Cardiff East Dock shed employed on pilot duties at Pengam on Sunday, 3rd March 1957. A lot of these engines had very short lives; this particular example enjoyed just short of ten years' service.

(Above) Plate 119 - Former Rhymney Railway Class R 0-6-2T No.35 (RR No.39) passing Glan-y-Llyn on Saturday, 10th November 1956 working the D10 Nantgarw Colliery-Cardiff Docks freight. The original Cardiff Railway station and goods shed for Glan-y-Llyn are visible at the rear of the train. No.35 was withdrawn from service in this month but in the following January was sent to Worcester for just over a year for use as a stationary boiler.

(Below) Plate 120 - 0-6-0PT No.9677 of East Dock shed employed on shunting duties at Pengam (Cardiff) on Sunday, 1st February 1953. Some idea of the amount of pilot and shunting duties undertaken by Cardiff East Dock shed can be gauged by looking at the number of 0-6-0PTs that were allocated to the depot.

Plate 121 - Former Rhymney Railway Class A1 0-6-2T No.66 (RR No.26) at Penrhos Junction with target D6, the 11.15am Penrhos Junction-Cherry Orchard empties on Friday, 3rd September 1954. Like most loose-coupled Down freights, D6 was required to stop at Wernddu for wagon brakes to be pinned down for the journey through Caerphilly Tunnel; they would then be lifted at Cefn On.

WORKING OF FREIGHT TRAINS - BARGOED PITS TO PENGAM.

● When a Down Freight Train leaves the Down Loop at Bargoed Pits Junction, the Guard may travel on the Engine from the Loop to Pengam Station in order to be at the leading end of the Train for the purpose of putting down brakes.

ENGINE AND VANS - PROPELLING BETWEEN BARGOED SOUTH SIGNAL BOX AND ABERBARGOED JUNCTION SIGNAL BOX AND VICE VERSA.

● An Engine may propel a Brake Van in the right direction over the Down Main Line between Bargoed South Signal Box and Aberbargoed Junction Signal Box, and also in the right direction over the Up Main Line between Aberbargoed Junction and Bargoed South Junction.

● The Guard must ride in the Brake van keeping a sharp lookout and be prepared to give any handsignal that may be necessary to the Driver. The Engine must proceed cautiously when propelling and the Driver be prepared to stop immediately in response to any fixed or hand signal. This working is prohibited during fog or falling snow.

● The maximum number that may be propelled is two Engines and two Brake Vans coupled.

WORKING BETWEEN PENGAM (MON.), ABERBARGOED JUNCTION0 AND BARGOED SOUTH WITH ASSISTING ENGINE.

● Traffic from Pengam and Britannia Collieries for Rhymney Section Down Line destinations may be worked from Pengam (Mon.) and Aberbargoed Junction to Bargoed South with the Assisting engine in front and the Train engine at the rear.

● Drivers of Train engines must not take water at Bargoed, nor must Drivers of Assisting Engines do so whilst engaged with these trains.

BARGOED STATION.

● During shunting operations at this Station all wagons brought from the Goods Shed Sidings must be shunted on to the Up Line only.

Plate 122 - Former Rhymney Railway Class R 0-6-2T No.42 (RR No.46) approaching Cefn On Halt with the D7 Roath Basin Junction-Bargoed Pits freight on Saturday, 31st March 1956. This was a much favoured location of Sid's as it offered good lighting and a raised background which fitted in well with his 'railways in the landscape' theme.

Plate 123 - Another former Taff Vale Railway locomotive allocated to Cardiff East Dock was Class O4 0-6-2T No.204 (TVR No.311) employed on shunting duties at Pengam on Thursday, 21st April 1955, three months before withdrawal. No.204 and No.290 bear the distinction of being the last members of the class to be withdrawn from service.

The start point or destination of numerous trains depicted were in the Docks, for which special arrangements applied:

CARDIFF DOCKS TRAFFIC WORKING ARRANGEMENTS.

● Traffic is worked between the undermentioned Storage Sidings and the Docks by Dock Executive Engines and Staff, namely:-
  Pengam Coal Sidings.
  Crockherbtown Sidings.
  Crwys Sidings.
● The Docks Engines carry distinctive discs having black numbers on a white ground fixed on the buffer planks.

● The limits of the Docks area are as under, viz.

Roath Branch	..	..	..	Reception Sidings Dock Storage North Box (exclusive).
Dock Branch	..	. .	..	Stonefield Junction Box (exclusive).
Rhymney Line	..	..	..	Tyndall Street Junction Box (exclusive).
Taff Vale Line	..	..	..	Cardiff Queen Street South (exclusive).

● Engines and men from the Cardiff Division, while working within the Docks area, are subject to the Rules and Regulations of the Docks Management, and controlled and supervised by the Docks Staff.
● Engines and men from the Docks, while working outside the Docks area, are subject to the Rules and Regulations of the Railway Section, and also the Special Regulations in the Appendices, and controlled and supervised by the Railway Staff.
● It is the duty of the Marshalling Inspector and Chief Dock Foreman, East Dock, to give to the Railway Sections as necessary at intervals each day advices of the coal necessary to cover the requirements of the Docks, and such coal must be given priority of conveyance.
● All Coal Trains from the various Storage Sidings to the Docks are worked by one Guard, who will be assisted by the Docks Staff in disposing of the traffic on the Hoist Roads or Sidings.
● Empty Colliery Wagons, as well as Pitwood Traffic, must, as far as possible, be marshalled by the Docks Engines and Staff.
● Information relating to the working of traffic and the requirements at the Docks, as well as the requirements at the Collieries in regard to empty wagons, pitwood, etc., must be fully and freely exchanged between the Docks and Railway Sections in order to secure the utmost efficiency and economy.

Plate 124 - 0-6-0PT No.3407 was in service for only six and a half years before being withdrawn and cut up at Caerphilly Works in the latter part of 1962. Here, the engine is turned onto the Down Relief at Heath Junction with a lengthy train of empties from Cherry Orchard to Cardiff Docks on Wednesday, 30th April 1958. This working was a Cardiff East Dock duty although the engine had been transferred from East Dock to Radyr the previous January.

Plate 125 - An Austerity style 0-6-0ST draws loaded wagons out of the colliery yard.

Industrial locomotives shunting at Llanbradach Colliery on Saturday, 27th April 1957

LLANBRADACH COLLIERY SIDINGS.

● Trainmen must ascertain that the gate across the line leading to the above Sidings is open before proceeding to or from the Colliery.

● A Notice Board is fixed 20 yards south of the Weighbridge house warning Trainmen not to lean out from the Engine cab when passing the Machine House.

NATIONAL COAL BOARD ENGINES WORKING ACROSS MAIN LINES AT LLANBRADACH.

● The N.C.B. Engines are allowed to work across the Railway at Llanbradach for the purpose of moving to and fro all traffic connected with the Colliery and Coal Washery, the movements being done at times convenient to Railway traffic and entirely under the direction of the Llanbradach Signalman.

COLLIERS' TRAINS FOR LLANBRADACH COLLIERY.

● Colliers' Trains for Llanbradach Colliery must be brought to a stand at the Colliery gate, from which point the Trains must not proceed until the Guard has received an assurance from the N.C.B.'s man who is deputed to meet the Train, or from personal observation, that the hand points are properly set and the road clear for the passage of the Train to the Coach Siding where the Colliers are detrained. If the Train is not met, the Guard must precede the Train on foot to the Coach Siding, and see that the hand points are properly set and the line clear for the passage of the Train.

● The speed of the Train over the Colliery's line must not exceed 4 miles per hour.

TRAINS WITH ASSISTING ENGINE IN REAR, LLANBRADACH TO PENALLTAU, ETC.

● Trains worked by two Engines from Llanbradach to Penalltau Junction, Bargoed Pits Junction, or intermediate points, must have the Assisting Engine in the rear, except where special instructions are given to the contrary, or when such Trains have full loads for points North of Bargoed Pits Junction, when the second engine must be attached in front throughout. In the case of three-engine loads, two engines must work in front and one in rear.

Plate 126 - 0-6-0ST 'LUNDIE', built by Andrew Barclay No.1091 in 1906, propels a train of pitprops towards the colliery.

CARDIFF CANTON

Originally constructed by the GWR, Canton shed was situated to the west of Cardiff General station on the site now occupied by the Diesel Depot and consisted of a roundhouse and a six-road dead-end shed. Its code was 86C, which was to become 88A on the 1st January 1961. Canton closed to steam on 9th September 1962, at which time all remaining steam locomotives were transferred to Cardiff East Dock shed.

In the winter of 1957/58, the shed was responsible for the working of 17 mineral and freight turns, described below.

Target No.	Start time	Start point, destination and notes + - Runs if required
H18	1.35am MX	Work to Radyr Junction
P1	6.0am	Work Penarth Curve to Sully
		(see note below)
H1	2.30am MX	Work to Rogerstone
	6.45am MO	Work to Newport (Dock Street)
H2	2.50am MX	Work Penarth Curve to Tondu
	3.40am MO	
H3	4.30am MX	Work to Barry
	5.40am MO	
H5	5.50am	Work to Radyr Junction
H6	8.10am	Work Penarth Curve to Llanharan
H8	8.0am	Work to Rogerstone
		(Runs if required on Saturdays)
H9	8.15am	Work to Peterston
		(to Llantrisant if required)
H18	8.20am	Work to Radyr Junction; Probably a double-turn; see H18 above
H11	10.30am	Work to Barry
---	1/0pm SX	Work to Ely
H15	2/30pm	Work to Rogerstone
H16	3/0pm	Work to Newport (Dock Street)
H17	2/40pm	Work Penarth Curve to Tondu
H19	5/55pm SX	Work to Rogerstone
H23	2.10am MX	Work to Newport (Dock Street)
	6/40pm SO	
H25	8/0pm	Work to Rogerstone

Locomotives allocated to Canton during 1957 included:

0-6-0PT No.1508
2-8-0 Nos.2813, 2821, 2837, 2859, 2864, 2867, 2874, 2877, 2891, 2892, 2893, 2895
0-6-0PT Nos.3670, 3755
2-8-0 Nos.3801, 3803, 3809, 3810, 3816, 3817, 3835, 3842, 3843, 3845, 3847, 3854, 3860
4-6-0 No.4073
2-8-0T Nos.4207, 4225, 4226, 4231, 4254, 4266, 4270, 4297
0-6-0PT Nos.4622, 4633
4-6-0 Nos.4934, 4946, 4964, 4968, 4973, 4974, 4996, 4999
4-6-0 Nos.5001, 5004, 5005, 5007, 5020, 5030, 5046, 5049, 5052, 5054, 5072, 5074, 5095, 5099
2-8-0T Nos.5207, 5218
2-6-0 No.5334
0-6-2T Nos.5602, 5633, 5679
4-6-0 Nos.5911, 5923, 5925, 5946, 5953, 5970, 5989
2-6-0 Nos.6308, 6333, 6338, 6352, 6353, 6362
0-6-2T Nos.6600, 6621, 6644
4-6-0 Nos.6928, 6932, 6939, 6943, 6946, 6948, 6958, 6969, 6998, 6999
4-6-0 Nos.7000, 7020, 7022, 7023
2-6-0 Nos.7322, 7328, 7332
0-6-0PT No.7775
0-6-0PT Nos.8429, 8439, 8441, 8447, 8457, 8464
0-6-0PT Nos.8723, 8728, 8776
0-6-0PT Nos.9426, 9437, 9443, 9450, 9459, 9461, 9477, 9493, 9494
0-6-0PT Nos.9603, 9648, 9713, 9723, 9759, 9778
4-6-2 Nos.70015, 70016, 70017, 70018, 70019, 70020, 70021, 70022, 70023, 70024, 70025, 70026, 70027, 70028, 70029
4-6-0 Nos.73014, 73024, 73025, 73026
4-6-0 Nos.75004, 75007, 75008, 75009, 75021, 75022
2-8-0 Nos.90125, 90148, 90188, 90201, 90238, 90312, 90323, 90524, 90565, 90572, 90579, 90693

*The **P1 duty** worked: 6.0am Penarth Curve North-Penarth, 8.53am Penarth-Grangetown (engine and brakevan), 10.20am Grangetown-Sully then 11.45am Sully-Grangetown, where it was due to arrive at 1/15pm. It was then up to the Control to arrange any further activity.*

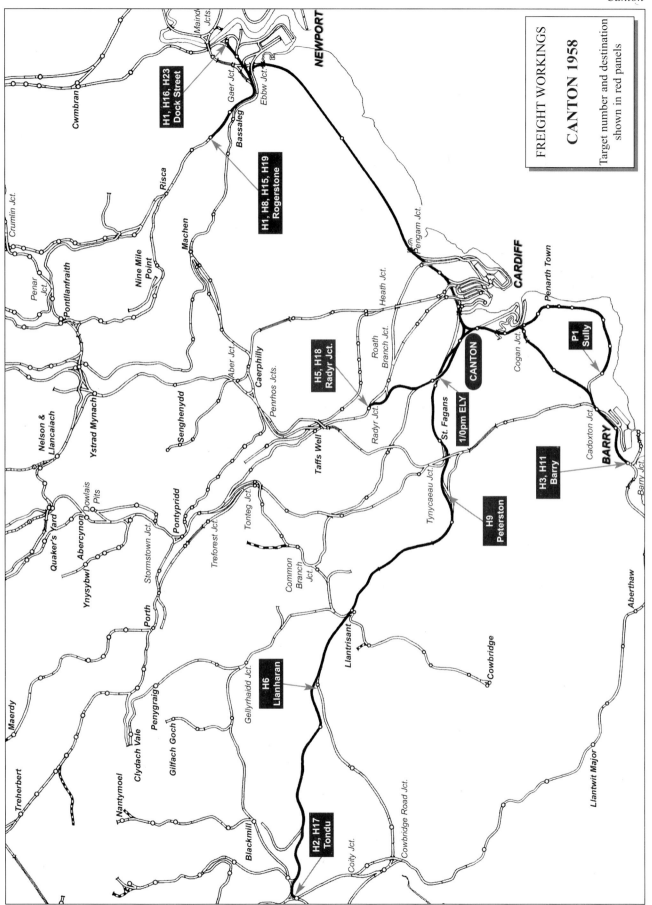

FREIGHT WORKINGS
CANTON 1958
Target number and destination shown in red panels

(Above) Plate 127 - 0-6-0PT No.3729 anives at Penarth Town station with the 10.20am Grangetown-Sully freight one summer's day in 1953. The trip was part of duty P1, the details of which are noted on page 98.

(Below) Plate 128 - 2-8-0T No.5207 of Canton near St.Fagans on the evening of Wednesday, 12th June 1957 with an eastbound Class F freight. With this particular stretch of line being relatively level, not a lot of steam would be needed to keep a fully laden train on the move, as demonstrated by No.5207's exhaust.

Canton

Plate 129 - A general view of the front of Cardiff Canton shed on Thursday, 1st September 1955 depicting former Alexandra (Newport & South Wales) Dock and Railway 2-6-2T No.1205 (ADR No.36) in use as shed pilot. No.1205 was the last remaining ADR engine in BR service and was withdrawn the following January having covered just short of half a million miles.

101

Plate 130 - *This is the same stretch of line as shown in the print of No.5382 (opposite) but looking the other way; in fact the Distant signal can be seen behind the fifth wagon. Here 2-8-0T No.4225 of Canton shed heads for Cardiff with an eastbound Class H freight c.1955.*

STEAM LOCOMOTIVE DEPOT, CANTON, CARDIFF.

● Outgoing engines for Cardiff West must travel via the East end of the shed to the Shed Starting Signal.
● Ingoing engines to the shed normally travel via Cardiff West.
● Two sidings situated at the rear of Canton Sidings Signal Box give access between the East and West end of the Steam Depot.
● The siding next to the Steam Locomotive Depot is known as No.1 Road and the one nearer the Signal Box as No.2 Road.
● Engines requiring to travel between the East and West ends of the Shed must do so over No.1 Road.

(Left) Plate 131 - *Former Taff Vale Railway somersault and revolving disc signals at Ely Paper Mills; Monday, 27th June 1955.*

Plate 132 - Canton-based 2-6-0 No.5382 near St. Georges with a westbound Class J freight on Saturday, 20th March 1954, six months before the locomotive would be reallocated to Ebbw Junction. In the background, on the left of the picture, is the former Barry Railway signal box at Tynycaeau Junction. The South Wales main line in this area is pretty uninspiring photographically but note how Sid has made use of the Distant signal and the railway line in the background to add interest to this shot.

(Above) Plate 133 - Canton's No.4225 at St. Fagans on Wednesday, 4th August 1954 with an Up troop train. Unusually for a 2-8-0T, No.4225 is displaying an express headcode and there appears to be some quite interesting Southern Region stock behind the locomotive. (Below) Plate 134 - Canton 2-8-0 No.2805 marshalling the stock of a Swansea to Paddington empty van train at Canton Sidings on Friday, 24th August 1956. Timings for these trains were lenient and a 2-8-0, which could get very lively on the footplate at anything approaching a medium speed, would experience no difficulties.

(Above) Plate 135 - A 94xx 0-6-0PT arriving at Ely (Main Line) station with the 8.42am Bridgend-Cardiff General stopping passenger train on Saturday, 4th April 1953. The slight haze from the chimney denotes good engine management by the Canton crew.

(Below) Plate 136 - At about 8.45pm on the evening of Wednesday, 12th June 1957, Canton-based 2-8-0T No.4254 approaches Ely with the H17 6/35pm Tondu-Penarth Curve North freight. This was the return working of the 2/40pm Penarth Curve North-Tondu empties.

(Above) Plate 137 - Barely a few months old, Hymek Bo-Bo diesel-hydraulic No.D7025, allocated from new to Canton, is at Platform 2 of Cardiff General heading the Up 'Red Dragon', the 10.0am Cardiff-Paddington express passenger train on Saturday, 7th July 1962. Note the small brackets above the locomotive number. They were for holding a small white plaque which displayed the engine driver's name and his home depot; not a popular practice as far as footplate men were concerned.

(Below) Plate 138 - Hall Class 4-6-0 No.4901 'Adderley Hall', of 86C, slows for the stop at Severn Tunnel Junction with the 12/6pm Port Talbot-Didcot, via Gloucester, stopping passenger train on Tuesday, 23rd July 1955. The journey time of this train was just over six and a half hours. To the right of the picture a 41xx 2-6-2T is shunting, whilst 2-6-2T No.5166, acting as pilot for 2-8-0 No.3850, wait to depart from the Up Yard with an eastbound freight.

Plate 139 - 2-8-0T No.4266 of Canton shed, which appears to be in a fairly clean condition and not long out of works, at the head of an eastbound Class H freight on Monday, 4th July 1955. Having just passed Pyle West Junction the locomotive crew will have no doubt prepared No.4266 for the climb up Stormy Bank's 1 in 93 gradient.

(Above) Plate 140 - Snow is on the ground as 0-6-0PT No.3642, allocated to Llanelli at the time, is employed on station pilot duties at Cardiff General on Thursday, 15th January 1959. The locomotive, in near ex-works condition, was probably working back to 87F after overhaul and would have been put on this Canton duty as a fill-in turn.

(Below) Plate 141 - A Swindon-built DMU heads for Cardiff and is about to cross the River Ely at St. Fagans on Friday, 7th June 1957. The guard's door on this nigh on brand new unit has been left open, so whether the unit was in revenue-earning service or crew training is not known. The BR Publicity Department produced posters stating that 'The NEW EXPRESS DIESEL SERVICES with Refreshment Facilities on the BIRMINGHAM-CARDIFF-SWANSEA route would commence on Monday, 17th June, 1957.'

(Above) Plate 142 - Canton 2-6-0 No.6333 passing through Ely with an Up Class J freight on Thursday, 5th February 1953. The railway passing overhead in the background is the line from Penarth Junction to Radyr Quarry Junction via Waterhall Junction. As well as freight traffic, the line was often used by passenger excursions to Ninian Park Halt and Barry Island.

(Below) Plate 143 - Another of Canton's 0-6-0PTs was No.9493 which is nearing Ebbw Junction with an Up train of empty coaching stock on Saturday, 23rd July 1955. The engine, not yet a year old, had been allocated to Canton from new and stayed there until July 1961 when it was transferred to Bromsgrove for use as a banking engine on the Lickey Incline.

(Above) Plate 144 - Back to one of Sid's favourite main line locations, the woodlands between St. Fagans and Ely. On Saturday, 14th May 1955 Canton's 2-8-0T No.4226 passes with an eastbound Class F freight. It was during that month that most train services were brought to a halt due to a rail dispute which dragged on for several weeks.

(Below) Plate 145 - 2-8-0T No.4231 of Canton on the Down Relief line near Rumney with a westbound Class H freight on Sunday, 22nd March 1953. No.4231, which looks in a quite clean condition, was allocated to 86C for many years and was withdrawn from the shed in December 1959.

Plate 146 - Making a vigorous departure from Llantrisant station is long-term Canton resident No.9723 with a Cardiff-Porthcawl stopping passenger train on Saturday, 13th July 1957. Sid's reason for being at Llantrisant was to photograph a visiting Stephenson Locomotive Society special with 0-4-2T No.1471 and 2-6-2T No.5574 as motive power at different times.

(Above) Plate 147 - The prestigious South Wales Pullman at Cardiff General on Wednesday, 11th July 1962. This was the 6.40am Swansea (High St.)-Paddington service with an arrival time of 10.15am. The return working left Paddington at 4.55pm and arrived at Swansea (High St.) at 8.40pm. Note that the driver had to wear a white cover over his greasetop hat.

(Below) Plate 148 - 0-6-0PT No.9713, at almost the same location as No.6333 in Plate 142, heading an eastbound freight through Ely on Monday, 23rd May 1955, during the period of the nationwide rail dispute. The trains that ran during this period were manned by crews who did not support the strike, but that resulted in many engines not being able to work the return journey to their home depot because of the shortage of footplate staff. However, that was not the case for Canton's No.9713.

Plate 149 - Canton 2-8-0 No.3824 has just passed Pyle West Junction on Wednesday, 7th April 1955 with an eastbound Class H freight. In the following September the locomotive would be reallocated to Ebbw Junction. Although No.3824 appears to be working hard, it is but a short distance from here before the engine would have to tackle Stormy Bank.

(Above) Plate 150 - Between St. Georges and St. Fagans on Friday, 20th February 1959 as 0-6-0PT No.4622 of Canton passes with a short Tondu-Penarth Curve Class J freight.

(Below) Plate 151 - One to puzzle over now. How did a Canton 0-6-0PT manage to work to Tredegar? This was certainly the case on Saturday, 8th August 1959 when No.5727 was photographed passing Tredegar No.1 signal box with a short Class K Down freight. The engine had been transferred from Severn Tunnel Junction to Canton in January 1958 and was withdrawn from service in May 1960.

INDEX

Plate 152 - Wishful thinking at Quaker's Yard; Thursday, 6th March 1958.